"From the first page to the last, it was so relatable that it took me back to Ranger Class 11-93 myself. No surprise, we all had the same journey to get to graduation day, sharing the same common bonds amongst us all. No one earns 'their' tab! #teamwork"

—Command Sergeant Major (Retired) Michael Evans, US Army

"It has been nearly twenty-eight years since I negotiated the Darby Queen, rucked the TVD, and waded the Florida swamps, but Nate's vivid description of those events, and all that comprises Ranger School, brought back a flood of memories! I could almost taste the blueberry pancakes in the mountains, the sawdust in the combative pit, and feel the weight of my rucksack all over again! *Roster Number Five-Zero* is a must read for anyone who has ever wanted to know what the US Army's premier leadership development school is really like—too easy!"

—Colonel (Retired) John Vermeesch, US Army

"One of the most outstanding and no-nonsense books about Ranger School that I have read in the last thirty-five years since I graduated. True and down-to-earth grit about what you have to do to finish such a grueling course."

—Command Sergeant Major (Retired) Jeffery Smith, US Army

"Nate's story takes you through the emotional spectrum of excitement, fear, disappointment, and finally exhilaration of becoming a US Army Ranger School graduate. Many service members volunteer, and with determination and luck, a select group earns the privilege and burden of becoming Ranger qualified."

—Major Roberto Lainez, US Army

"Nate Aguinaga did it again. This time sharing his gripping personal accounts of his rigorous and emotional journey through one of the most mentally and physically demanding schools within the US Army. If you want a book that you won't stop reading, this is it!"

—Colonel John Schwemmer, US Army, Infantry

"A follow-up to *Division,* this is a must read for anyone aspiring to better understand what it takes to graduate from one of the Army's most demanding leadership courses. In *Roster Number Five-Zero,* Nate provides an honest, unvarnished perspective of how Ranger School's grueling hardships forge soldiers into the Army's finest leaders and prepare them for the rigors of combat."

**—Lieutenant Colonel (Retired) Jeff Robertson, US Army,
Ranger Class 01-96**

"Nate has done it again. I graduated Ranger School four days before jumping into Panama in Dec '89, and I felt like we were in the same class. As I read the book, I was thrust back in time and felt the experience all over again. I laughed, smiled and even cursed out loud. . . . Rangers Lead the Way!"

—Sergeant Major (Retired) Marvin Gardner, US Army

Roster Number Five-Zero
by Nathan Aguinaga

ISBN 978-1-64663-085-1

Published by

 köehlerbooks™

3705 Shore Drive
Virginia Beach, VA 23455
800–435–4811
www.koehlerbooks.com

ROSTER NUMBER FIVE-ZERO

NATHAN AGUINAGA

VIRGINIA BEACH
CAPE CHARLES

TABLE OF CONTENTS

Not for the weak or fainthearted

"Let the enemy come till he's almost close enough to touch. Then let him have it and jump out and finish him with your hatchet."

Major Robert Rogers, 1759

RANGER TRAINING BRIGADE

United States Army Infantry School Fort Benning, Georgia

FOREWORD

T hose who've attempted US Army Ranger School are forever scarred by the experience. Whether they made it through and wear the coveted Ranger tab or not, they will carry the memories of that experience for the remainder of their days. If you want to learn about Ranger School, one of the United States military's toughest, there are plenty of documentaries you can watch and numerous writings which describe the challenge. In these pieces you will learn of Ranger School's phases, you'll see students looking gaunt, struggling to overcome, and you'll connect with its instructors as they describe the course.

None of this, however, will give you the real, behind-the-scenes story like this book. Through his raw, unadulterated prose and vibrant storytelling, Nate Aguinaga gives the reader a Ranger School "backstage pass." You'll get it NCO-style. In his unique "Agui" way, you'll feel like you're having a beer with him as he reveals his stories of hardship and perseverance. Enter "zero dark thirty" and experience the worm pits, obstacle courses and beaten pavement of Fort Benning. Rig up and parachute into the jungles of the Florida Panhandle. Navigate the punishing inclines of the Tennessee Valley Divide or stand at parade rest as a heartless Ranger instructor decides your fate.

Like his last book, Nate carried me back, almost thirty years, to my time in hell. My chest tightened, my stomach turned in knots and I even grew hungry and fatigued. I could smell the burning of muscle tissue, feel the coarseness and strength of 550 parachute cord and weight of that heavy pack and even taste the blueberry pancakes. I laughed as I recalled my own suffering and small moments of joy amidst such misery. I could hear the F-bombs and feel the resentment Nate felt toward a school and its instructors which throws the book at you. I immediately gravitated toward and was entertained by Nate's "grunt-style" vernacular. Captivated, I couldn't put the book down. Be Nate's Ranger Buddy and travel this journey with him in the pages ahead. You'll feel his angst, anger, relief and final triumph as he dons the black-and-gold patch and earns the title Army Ranger, a title so many strive to attain. Are you ready, Ranger? Ready to take a journey through one of our nation's toughest schools? It's not for the weak or fainthearted. What are you going to do now, Ranger?!! Turn the page.

—**Colonel (Retired) Rob Campbell, Army Ranger**
Author, *It's Personal, Not Personnel: Leadership Lessons for the Battlefield and the Boardroom* and *At Ease: A Soldier's Story and Perspectives on the Journey to an Encore Life and Career*

INTRODUCTION

Make no mistake about it. This is not a documentary on US Army Ranger School. This is not a technical manual on equipment or a field manual on Infantry tactics either. If you want to read about these tasks, I suggest purchasing or downloading a Ranger Handbook or Field Manual 7-8: The Infantry Platoon and Squad. Therefore, I ask the readers to be a little tolerant of my memory on tactics, techniques, and procedures during my time in Ranger School. I've been "out of the game" for a while now, since my retirement after twenty years in the Army in 2010. I may even be out of order of events during certain days, especially during my memories of Ranger Assessment Phase. So, if you are a fellow Ranger and/or infantryman, please bear with me on certain specifics of this spin-off of my first book, *Division: Life on Ardennes Street.*

This is my personal account of my experience in one of the hardest leadership combat-training courses throughout all of the military branches of the Armed Forces—US Army Ranger School. Although the duration and the phases have been altered, decreased, and extended throughout the almost seventy years that Army Ranger School has existed, one aspect has never changed: It is a very physically and mentally difficult military course with an extremely high attrition rate. Candidates of Ranger School will undergo evaluations while leading combat patrols under extreme weather, terrain, and physical conditions, to include sleep deprivation and starvation. During the sixty-two-day course (when you add in "zero day"), the average Ranger student will receive approximately two to three hours of sleep in a twenty-four-hour period, and will lose between twenty to thirty pounds by graduation day.

This book covers my time as a Ranger student in the fall of 2003. Not only will I discuss the everyday difficulties that the course offers, but also the personal hardships that many students, including myself, face during almost every class. These personal hardships consist of personality differences between students and some of the instructors during each of the three phases of training. I will talk about how the students can easily turn on their own peers very quickly and also how the instructors can turn on a student if they perceive that there is a conflict between that student and their authority.

When I say "perceive," that means that if a misunderstanding between a student and an instructor occurs, as happened to me, it could be detrimental towards the student moving on to the next phase, even after possibly being recycled in the phase they are in. If that occurs, there's a likelihood that the student may never be afforded the chance to move on; that they may be "targeted" by the Ranger instructors (RIs) of that particular platoon or company they are assigned to. These are the realities of this course that are not shown on the few documentaries that exist on *Discovery Channel* or *National Geographic* on US Army Ranger School.

CHAPTER 1

ZERO DAY

When I attended Ranger School in 2003, Army policy was that every Ranger student must have successfully completed a pre-Ranger course back at their home base or at Fort Benning, where Ranger School is headquartered, begins, and ends. The exception was, and probably still is to this day, that if you were an Infantry senior noncommissioned officer that graduated from the Advanced Noncommissioned Officer's Academy (ANCOC), you could walk onto Ranger School. The same exception applied to graduates of the Infantry Officer's Basic Course (IOBC) for new Infantry Branch lieutenants.

I graduated ANCOC in September 2003, and instead of going back to Fort Bragg, North Carolina, my current duty station at the time, I stayed on Fort Benning to start Ranger School two days later. I had just been promoted a month earlier, while in ANCOC, to sergeant first class (E-7) and I was thirty-one. The average enlisted rank of a Ranger student is E-4 or E-5, with an average age of twenty-three years old. Obviously, I was considered an "old man" going through the course. I damn sure didn't feel like it, though, because I was in the best shape of my life. I was 170 pounds and pretty cut up from working out every day to prepare for Ranger School during my three months in ANCOC. After class my friends would go get a few beers and dinner at Hooters, and instead, I would make myself go to the gym for two hours every day. Make no mistake about it, I did "play" and let loose from time to time. My workout routine was Monday through Friday lifting weights and running on the treadmill in the gym behind Olsen Hall, where the ANCOC and IOBC students stayed. Saturdays, I would throw my rucksack on my back with boots on and take myself on a four or five-mile foot march around Benning. Most Sundays I would take off and relax.

I drove myself to Camp Rogers around 3 a.m., with a report time of 4. There were about four or five other ANCOC graduates reporting there along with me, so we huddled together in the parking lot until we were called over to enter one of the buildings. Camp Rogers was as old as Ranger School itself. Most of the buildings were the old-style steel-arched Quonset huts. Once inside, we were told to take a seat and fill out the green cards they handed out to us. There were no tables. We sat on the floor and filled out our green cards as fast as we could because the RIs were yelling at us to hurry up and get outside to form up for the Ranger physical fitness test (PT test). The cards we were filling out are mandatory for every student who walks through the door on zero day of Ranger School. It asks name, rank, social security number, unit of assignment, and how many attempts this is for each student going through this course. Supposedly, it is kept on file for eternity at Ranger Training Brigade (RTB) in order to maintain a record for every servicemember that starts the school, which is open for all branches of the military, not just the Army.

We were told to go get our two duffle bags and stack them to the side of the building we had just left and to stand by. We were then marched to the hand-to-hand combat pit across the street from the buildings of Camp Rogers, where we would be conducting the fitness test. The standard to pass the test was fifty-two push-ups in two minutes, sixty-two sit-ups in two minutes, run two miles under fourteen minutes and fifty seconds, and six dead-hang pull-ups immediately after the run. I'll admit that I was anxious and nervous about taking the Ranger PT test due to the "hype" leading up to this point. Hype that had been built up over years of horror stories from guys that were Ranger qualified back at Bragg. Listening to them, you would have thought that this PT test was virtually impossible to pass. In fact, it was just the opposite for me, as I focused on it one event at a time.

I knocked out my fifty-two push-ups without having to repeat, and the same went for the sit-ups. I knocked out the run in great time and got in one of the dozens of lines for the pull-ups. You couldn't use your legs to kick or move any part of your lower body for momentum to assist pulling your chin over the bar. The RI grading you would say, "Mount the bar, Ranger." Once you were free-hanging, with your elbows locked, he would give the command, "Begin, Ranger." Once your chin was over the bar, you came down until your elbows were locked again, and then he would count the repetition, "One." You did that six times and the PT test was over. He then told me to move to the formation on the left side. The other formation on the right was for failures. Every student was afforded two chances to pass each event. For example, if one failed the push-ups twice, they were out of the course. As I stood in the "passing formation," I glanced over to the "non-passing formation," and there appeared to be about twenty students that failed the test. I remember saying to myself at that point, "There's nothing that's going to stop me now." I wasn't worried about the upcoming swim test, which was the other mandatory event you had to pass to get through zero day of Ranger School.

After the last of the students were complete with the pull-ups, we were instructed to go to our duffle bags and change into BDUs (battle dress uniform), boots, and a patrol cap. Every student was to have a two-quart canteen of water strapped around our necks as well. There was no changing area provided; it was right there, bare ass out in the open in front of God and everybody. We were instructed to pack another set of BDUs, an additional pair of boots, and another

T-shirt. We were to pack them in a wet-weather bag and get on one of the two or three buses that were parked outside of the camp. We headed for Main Post to one of the swimming pools as the sun was just coming up. The swimming pool was right across from Airborne School, and on the other side of the 200-foot towers, which were a pretty famous and common sight on Fort Benning.

As the bus pulled out of Camp Rogers, I noticed the PT failures sitting on their duffle bags, awaiting dismissal from the course. One of them was a fellow student from my ANCOC class. I remember looking out the window at him thinking that perhaps he should have worked out a little more while at the academy, rather than worrying about the "party lifestyle," but I was not judging. At this point of zero-day testing, I only needed to worry about my own ass.

The ride to Main Post was an irritating one. The students from the 75th Ranger Regiment were young and obnoxious. They were singing the whole way to Main Post, which was about a twenty to twenty-five-minute ride. The songs they were singing were old military chants. When I think back, it was sort of funny because these were young Infantry soldiers that treated Ranger School like it was a retreat away from their difficult units. Most of them, if not all, had already served at least one combat tour in Afghanistan by this time. Ranger battalion boys, or as the rest of the Army simply referred to them, "Bat Boys," were the equivalent of the young Marine mentality of "nobody can compare to us" within the Army itself. So, the majority of us maintained our sanity on the bus ride to the Combat Water Survival Test (CWST) while these young "gung-ho warriors" sang their songs in cheer and celebration. Again, I think they were celebrating the fact that they were away from the stresses of their elite units, rather than celebrating that they had just passed the Ranger School PT test.

When we arrived at the outdoor pool, the RIs had us file into the locker room and set our wet-weather bags on the benches and then move outside to the pool. The water test consisted of three events. The high drop, where the student is blindfolded and walks to the end of a diving board wearing BDUs, boots, load-carrying equipment (LCE), and carrying a rubber duck, which is a slang term soldiers call a fake or simulated M16 assault rifle. Once at the end of the diving board, the student must step forward, about five meters above the water, while holding the weapon straight out in front of them. The student then steps off the board on command of the RI, falling into the water without letting go of the weapon. If they drop the weapon when submerged in the water, they must repeat the event again. If they fail it twice, they're dropped from the course. Same standard as the PT Test; if they fail any of the three CWST events twice, they're dropped.

The next event, and not in this particular order, is the backwards drop. The student leaps into the water backwards from the side of the pool, again into the deep end. While underwater, they must remove their equipment (LCE and weapon) and swim away from it. When they reemerge to the surface, they must have their equipment separated from their bodies.

The final event, and the one that causes the most failures of the CWST, is the fifteen-meter swim with LCE and weapon. Each student must swim the distance with their heads and the barrel of the weapon above water. Weak swimmers usually will fail this event as they may begin to panic and move to the side of the pool or drop their weapon and reach for the side. If they touch the side of the pool at all, they are an automatic failure for that event. We lost another twenty to twenty-five students on the CWST. Altogether, by around 11 a.m. when we finished the CWST and got back on the buses, out of approximately 200 students that started that morning, about 50 were already failures and out of Ranger School. Out of the four or five other fellow ANCOC graduates that I showed up with, I was the only one left before noon on zero day, which was not over by far.

The bus ride back to Camp Rogers was even more obnoxious than it was earlier when we came to Main Post. The Bat Boys were singing their songs and playing grab-ass games again. I swear if I didn't know any better, I'd have thought they were on a fucking vacation. They were like little kids just arriving at summer camp, away from their parents for the first time. It's funny when I look back at it today.

I sat next to this guy who just looked at me and shook his head at all the noise the Bat Boys were making. I asked him where he was from in the Army. He was coming from Germany, assigned to a reconnaissance unit—more specifically, E Company, 51st Long Range Surveillance Detachment (LRSD). He looked and acted a little older, so I asked him what his rank was. In Ranger School, the students must strip their uniforms of rank, unit insignia and all special skill badges in order to have zero identity other than last name and US Army, or whatever branch of the military they belonged to. All heads must also be shaven bald prior to showing up on zero day.

He happened to be a staff sergeant (E-6), and this too was his first time attending Ranger School. So, he and I shot the shit on the bus ride back to camp and got along right off the bat. I told him if we ended up in the same platoon, we could be "Ranger buddies." Every student must have a Ranger buddy throughout the duration of the sixty-two-day course. He said, "Hell yeah, that's cool." I had met my first friend in Army Ranger School on zero day.

When we got back to Camp Rogers, the chaos began. "Rangers, get your asses off the buses, put your wet-weather bags over by your duffle bags, and get the fuck back here in formation! Swim test No-Gos, sit on your duffle bags and stand by for further instructions! I'm not telling you what to do with your wet gear, Rangers, but if it were me, I'd pull that shit out and lay it on your duffle bags so it can dry out! Now hurry the fuck up and get into formation; we got training to start!"

After laying out our wet BDUs and boots, we formed up and were marched across the road back to the hand-to-hand pit. I remember looking up at the entrance of the pit area, which was pretty intimidating because there were two large, towering utility-pole logs with a huge Ranger Tab hanging in the center of them. We got pretty used to seeing this pit and got very familiar with it over the next five days and nights.

We were in a column formation, and one of the RIs got out in front and commanded, "File from the left, follow me, Rangers!" We filed into the pit at a double time and jogged around for about fifteen to twenty minutes in a single-file line. Our two-quart canteens were slung across our bodies, and we were told to drink water whenever we wanted to, without having to be told when to do so—just don't stop running while you drink.

One of the RIs hollered out, "Quick time, Rangers! Walk it off!" We walked around the pit for about two laps and were told to stop and face the center. Two RIs jumped on the demonstration platform in the center of the pit and began our first block of instruction, which was our first hand-to-hand takedown drill. They weren't bullshitting; we were going right into training. I guess any in-processing we were going to do was totally complete when we filled out that green card at 0400 that morning.

The instructors would demonstrate each drill and then turn it over to us to practice and then go full force on one another. All of us were paired off—not chosen by the RIs, but random or whoever was closest to us. After doing each hand-to-hand move a few times on one another, we would be instructed to run around the pit. We would switch off from having to "bear crawl" and then conduct buddy carries when told to do so. This went on for the next few hours.

"Let's go, Rangers, move your asses! This shit is just beginning! None of you should be tired yet! If you are feeling tired, you might be in the wrong fucking school, Rangers—move it!"

I remember thinking that I would sure like to eat something, since my last meal was dinner the evening prior, and it was already about 1600. Lo and behold, we were finally instructed to exit the pit and form up. On the way to forming up we were told to stop off at the water buffalo and top off our canteens.

"We're going to eat chow, Rangers!"

The formation cheered like we were at the Super Bowl. We marched back onto the camp and straight to the mess hall. Outside, we were taught the Ranger School standard of entering any mess hall during any of the three phases. Six students would volunteer to step in front of the formation, and each would sound off with a portion of the Ranger Creed, and the rest of us would echo that portion, until the entire Ranger Creed was complete. Afterwards, each student would move to a row of pull-up bars and knock out six pull-ups before entering the chow line inside the dining facility. Again, this would be the standard during the entire sixty-two-day course.

Now, I've heard all the urban legends and/or horror stories of previous students saying that their initial chow hall meals in Ranger School were simply chaotic, and that the students were not even allowed to sit down and eat their meals. Instead, they were to eat as much as they could while walking their trays to the trash cans and then get outside. Another rumor I heard from past students was that the RIs would force you to eat your whole tray of food, and then take you outside and "smoke" everyone until they all threw up.

I will say that I did not experience this. My initial meal at Camp Rogers, we were afforded the opportunity to sit down and eat our dinner chow. I'm not calling those that have told these stories liars, but am just saying that I did not experience that. However, we could not sit there and just shoot the shit, but rather had to eat our meal in its entirety, then hurry up and get out to formation, like any other military school. I believe that first Ranger School meal was chili mac, and it was the best chili mac I'd ever eaten in my entire life.

After chow, it was back to the hand-to-hand pit for more training, more bear crawls, more buddy carries, push-ups, flutter kicks, etc. Simply put, a continuous series of "ass-smokings" well into the night and literally into the next morning. It was well after midnight when we finished in the pit for zero day. We formed up and marched back across the street, and were told to secure our duffle bags, which had been in the same spot since 0400 the morning prior. We thought they were going to take us to our barracks and bed us down for the night. Unfortunately, we were gravely mistaken.

There were about 140 of us remaining from a little over 200 that started that morning. One of the RIs marched us over to the headquarters building and told us to relax, drink water, and to check out the rosters on the bulletin board outside the main entrance. They covered what our roster numbers were, and our company and platoon of assignment. They broke us down into two companies— Alpha and Bravo. Within each company, they broke us down into two platoons. The RI came back out and told us to get a leader for each company and one each for the platoons.

"Don't worry about platoon sergeants and squad leaders at this time, Rangers. That'll come later, as I'm sure y'all are aware of. Right now, for Assessment Phase Week, we only want to contact a company commander and/or a platoon leader. So, figure out who they're gonna be by the time I get back out to you in about ten minutes, Rangers. Also, you all need to get a Ranger buddy that's assigned to the same platoon. So, your task, Rangers, is to have two companies, four platoons with a company commander, a platoon leader for each, and everybody has a Ranger buddy. See you in ten minutes, Rangers."

That was easy. Me and my buddy from Germany ended up in the same platoon, so we were officially Ranger buddies. I believe actual officers stepped up for the initial leadership roles required for the upcoming assessment phase.

When the RI came back out, we were still all standing around in a gaggle. He didn't take a great liking to that, so he told us to get on our backs for about another ten minutes of flutter kicks.

"Let's go, Rangers! Get up, and get your asses in the four platoons according to these rosters and give me a fucking leader standing in front of each. Move! We're on your time now, Rangers! You can get three hours of sleep or an hour. It don't make any difference to me. I'll be here all night anyway, Rangers." We got into four platoon formations, but it was sloppy, and some students had already forgotten which one they were to get into. The sleepiness and disorientation were starting to set in for some of the students.

"Stop, Rangers, just stop! Get on your backs and start fluttering again. We'll stay out here until the next formation, which will be in about three and a half hours, Rangers! It don't mean two shits to me!" After about another ten minutes he yelled out, "OK, get up and let's try this again. Move!" By now it was going on 0200. We got into our proper formations, and he seemed to be satisfied with our promptness.

"Alright, Rangers; Alpha Company, you're in the barracks on the right, and Bravo on the left. Take your duffle bags, find a wall locker and bunk and get some rest, Rangers. 0500 formation right back here. BDUs, PT belt, and running shoes. You all have your five-mile run, so keep drinking water, Rangers. Platoon leaders, make sure you put together a fire guard roster for your barracks. Anybody got any questions before I release you, Rangers?"

Of course, in every military school, in every class, there's always one dumbass that raises their hand, and we had one right at that moment.

"Yeah, what do you got for me, Ranger?"

The dumbass's question was, "Sergeant, when do we draw linen for our bunks?" Usually, in most military schools, a set of linen consisted of a pillow, a pillowcase, a set of sheets, and two blankets. Everybody sighed out loud. We were all like, "What the fuck?!"

The RI gave him a confused look, probably in disbelief that someone would ask such a thing in this course. Hell, we were appreciative of having a mattress to lie on at all.

"Ranger, who the fuck do you think I am—Martha fucking Stewart? Get back on your backs, Rangers. This night is not over!" We did another fifteen minutes of flutter kicks. At around 0230, zero day of Ranger School was over for us, twenty-two and a half hours after we signed in.

I was Roster Number Five-Zero, and we had sixty-one days to go before graduation.

CHAPTER 2

RANGER ASSESSMENT PHASE (RAP WEEK)

R AP Week was a five-day pass-or-fail series of events that each student must complete successfully in order to actually begin Ranger School. These tasks consisted of day and night land navigation, a five-mile run, a two-man buddy run in combat equipment, a water confidence course, a bayonet assault course, an obstacle course, weapons and communications testing, more hand-to-hand combat classes, Airborne Refresher Day with a parachute jump, and finally, a fifteen-mile road march from Camp Rogers out to Camp Darby.

Our first formation was at 0500 back at the headquarters building. We wore BDUs, PT reflector belt, and tennis shoes. The RIs came out and took accountability of us by calling out our roster numbers. Lo and behold, a couple of students were not in formation. They must have left sometime during our full two and half hours of sleep. The RI that was on duty during the time that we bedded down came out and said to the other instructors that two had signed out about two hours ago, shortly after we went to our barracks.

"Alright, Rangers, strip off your BDU tops and secure your PT belts around your waists, and ground your two-quarts." We stretched out for about ten minutes before knocking out the five-mile run. The standard was to run it in formation at an eight-minute-mile pace—to be completed in forty minutes. We took off and did just that. The instructors kept us right at the pace. They must have done this a time or two. It was a pretty simple run to complete, if you were in great shape. If you made it this far on day one, you were just that—in prime physical condition.

We finished the run, fell back onto our two-quarts and BDU tops, and were told to stretch out on our own to keep our muscles from tightening up. Then we heard the good news.

"Platoon leaders, march them to the chow hall, conduct the Ranger Creed, pull-ups, and get them inside for breakfast." We all cheered again, like someone just told us we had won the lottery and were instant millionaires. There was a pattern beginning that we all quickly realized, and it became a standard for our class, and probably for every class before ours as well. When the RIs told us we were going to the dining facility, it was free game to cheer as loud as we could.

After chow, a quick shower, and clean BDUs, it was on the buses back to Main Post for TA-50 issue—our tactical gear, such as helmets, LCE items, and large rucksacks. Oh yeah, there was plenty more singing and grab-ass games from the Bat Boys on the way there. I looked at my Ranger buddy from Germany and said to him, "Well, the first RAP Week task is over, brother." Meaning the five-mile run.

He high-fived me and replied, "Hell yeah, too easy, dude." That soon became our saying to one another after each mandatory task was complete—"Too easy."

When we got back to Camp Rogers, they had us secure our TA-50 in our wall lockers and hurry back out for formation. It was time to march back across the street for more hand-to-hand training and ass-smokings for the rest of the day and well into the night. We did get dinner chow in between. At this point, we were counting meals, and thus far, we ate three meals in the past sixty hours we had been in the course.

The hand-to-hand combat classes were extensive and brutal at times. We were not allowed to "sugarcoat" any of the takedowns or body throws. This was the old hand-to-hand techniques, prior to the Brazilian-style Jiu Jitsu that became the Army combatives standard shortly afterwards. As a matter of fact, we were told that we were one of the last classes that would get the twenty to twenty-five hours of the "old-style" combatives sessions in Ranger School. The new-style Jiu Jitsu combatives classes were more of a wrestling technique that emphasized choke holds and arm bar movements. Either way, they were long, extensive hours that went well into the night. When we finished training for the night and got back out in front of the headquarters, it was well after 0100 again.

"Rangers, put your LCEs and rucksacks together according to the standards posted on the bulletin board. Formation will be 0430, Rangers. BDUs, boots, patrol caps, rucksacks with a dry set of BDUs and boots inside one of your wet-weather bags. Make sure you have your reflective belts around your rucks, Rangers. Get to work on your equipment. PLs, when they're complete with their equipment, they can go nighty-night." There was no timeline or training schedule posted. We went off of whatever time and uniform they told us a few hours earlier. Only the instructors knew what was next on the agenda. So, that made it a little more mind boggling—the not knowing. You had to make yourself just go through each event as told to do so, because at the end of the day, we were just trying to make it out of this course successfully with a Ranger Tab. Day one of RAP Week ended around 0200 again, and there were sixty days until graduation. Too easy.

Day two (actually day three if you count zero day) started out with a cool, brisk morning, and about a two-mile hike to Victory Pond. We figured it was going to be the "dreaded" Ranger School water confidence course because the RI a few hours prior told us to pack a set of BDUs and boots in our rucks. I told Germany that we were headed to the infamous water course and he agreed. From here on out, I will refer to my new Ranger buddy as Germany, and honestly, not just for privacy purposes, but because I forgot his damn name and roster number. Give me a break; it was some time ago, and I've been through a lot, and have interacted with so many soldiers since then. Anyway, we looked at each other, and admitted a little nervousness, but convinced one another that it was a Band-Aid that simply needed to be ripped off. In other words, "Let's get this shit over with."

When we arrived to Victory Pond, we grounded our equipment in formation and moved over for a briefing and a demonstration by the instructors. The sun was just coming over the tree line in the distance, and it was still cool outside. After the demonstrations, they moved us over to draw life vests and then sent each of our two companies to the two separate events. The evaluations began immediately; they never wasted our time on this or any other event during RAP Week. I had to do the slide-for-life event first. We climbed up a seventy-foot metal ladder to the top and proceeded to a platform with an RI giving guidance on when to execute the task. I'll admit, when I got to the top, it seemed as if I had climbed 200 feet, but that's probably because we were tired and hungry.

Anyway, the RI said, "Alright, Ranger, move forward to the platform." Once I was there, he gave me the order, "Execute, Ranger." You had to jump up and a little bit forward to grab the bar, and once you did, away you went with a pretty decent speed down towards the water. The standard was, when you saw the RI below wave the red flag, you were to release from the bar and enter the water. It was more like a slam into the water because you were coming down so fast from so high up.

We then swam over to a ladder on the bank and got out of the water, just to hurry up and get into the line for the next event, which was the dreaded beam walk. This event was the one with all the horror stories. You climbed up a thirty-five-foot ladder. Once on top, you had to walk across a wooden beam that was about the width of a railroad tie. Halfway across the beam was a little platform that you had to step up and over, without using your hands at all. Once on the other side, you continued to walk the remainder of the beam until you got to a rope that was horizontal, still thirty-five feet in the air. You had to shimmy across the rope until you got to a two-foot-long, wooden Ranger Tab, touch the tab, and then release your legs from the rope. Once suspended by your hands and arms, you had to ask the RI who was grading you for permission to drop into the water.

"Roster Number Five-Zero, request permission to drop, Sergeant!"

He replied, "Drop, Ranger!"

You released the rope and plunged into the frigid water. If any student showed signs of fear of heights or hesitation to calmly go through either of these two events, they were dropped from the course. Fear of heights or water was definitely a showstopper in Ranger School, especially with Mountain and Florida Phases coming up, but we'll get into that later.

Once done, I reported to the RI, and he confirmed that I was a "Go" on both events, and said to go to my ruck and put on dry BDUs, T-shirt, socks, and boots. Again, it was bare-ass naked, changing in front of God and everybody. I got done before Germany. When he linked up with me over by our rucks, I asked him if he was good. He gave me a sarcastic look and said, "Ah, dude, too easy."

I replied, "Oh, fuck yeah it was—way too easy." The reality was that an hour ago we were both nervous as fuck.

We got back to Camp Rogers, and it was only about 1000 hours. We were hoping they would march us to the chow hall, but that did not happen. No breakfast. Instead, we were told to secure our helmets, LCEs, and leather gloves. We emptied out our wet clothes and strung them up on the 550 cord we had outside our barracks in order to dry. We then formed back up on the street.

The instructors marched us down the road to the Bayonet Assault Course. It was your typical training on using a bayonet attached to rubber ducks. They took us through the basic bayonet training on stabbing moves and butt strokes with our weapons. Once that was complete, each student ran the course himself. The only big thing I remember during this mandatory training was how hot it was outside and that we were covered with mud from head to toe after we were complete. I believe today bayonet training is no longer a part of RAP Week or Ranger School. Other than Basic Training, I don't think the Army trains on it at all anymore. I don't see how you could, due to all the attachments one has on their individual weapon anyway. How the hell could you attach a bayonet with all the shit on your M-4?

Back outside our barracks we hosed off our equipment and got all the mud off everything. We hung up our wet equipment from the bayonet course, and changed back into the now-dry BDUs that were hanging up from this morning. We formed back up with dry BDUs—not clean, but dry—and our two-quarts.

"It's chow time, Rangers!" Cheers and more cheers. We marched to the dining facility for our fourth meal in three days.

After chow, it was back across the street for another evening of beloved hand-to-hand combat training and ass-smokings. I remember they cut this session off earlier than normal. Come to find out, the special occasion was an earlier night for an earlier morning. Formation the next morning was around 0300 outside the building where we initially filled out our green cards. Uniforms were going to be BDUs, LCEs, and patrol caps for land navigation. The RIs actually released us around 2330 for three and a half hours before the next day started. I remember taking a hot shower and getting into clean BDU bottoms and T-shirt with clean, fresh socks for bed. No pillow, sheets, or blankets, just my poncho liner or what we call our "wooby," and I would roll up another set of BDUs for my pillow. Again, we simply appreciated being able to lie down for a few hours on a mattress. Fifty-nine days until graduation.

About three and a half hours later we were inside the same building we started in. We lay on the floor with the maps we were issued, plotting out our points we had to find on the maps for day and night land navigation, the next mandatory event we had to pass to continue on in the course. The standard was to find seven out of nine points (I believe, if my memory serves me correctly) using a map and a compass. The course was to begin at 0500 and be completed by 0900, the logic being there would be two hours of darkness and then two hours of daylight to locate all nine points. We were allowed to have on us a red-lensed flashlight, only to be used to assist reading our map and to mark our point once we located it. If you were caught using it to navigate, or caught talking to another student, you were dropped from the course for integrity purposes. This was one of those tasks that would knock out a handful of students from Ranger School. I learned a long time ago during these land navigation tests to remain calm, trust in your compass, plotting techniques, your 100-meter pace-count, and definitely walk straight-line distance through whatever terrain you have to. Stay off the roads and/or firebreaks. If any student failed their first time, I believe they were allotted a second chance to retest.

Germany and I both received Gos for the land-navigation event. We looked at each other before we got back on the buses to head back and said, "Too easy." He even gave me a "Ppfff, way too easy." One thing was for sure, my confidence was increasing more and more as these events came and went with success. However, I had to continuously remind and encourage myself that I was an experienced infantryman with twelve years of service, that I should have no problem passing these events with no excuses; however, I needed to remain humble, and not get cocky whatsoever.

When we got back to camp we were sent to breakfast, and then more training afterwards. Each of the four platoons were split off, and we went with our assigned RIs. We went behind headquarters and were told to take a seat in the grass, and we received our first class on combat orders. The first one was a long, drawn-out class on writing a five-paragraph operations order.

"Pull out your Ranger Handbooks and note-taking material, Rangers. This is a very important class that you are about to receive, and it is going to be your 'bread and butter' for the planning portions of every single mission you will go on during the duration of this course, Rangers. Therefore, it would behoove you to stay awake and pay attention to what you get from this block of instruction. If everybody starts falling asleep, Rangers, we'll just say fuck it, and take you over across the street and do some more hand-to-hand instead, so that you can wake your asses up. So, stand your asses up if you find yourselves falling asleep."

One thing I noticed about Ranger School so far was that there wasn't a whole lot of screaming at the students. The RIs, for the most part, were calm and gave clear, concise instructions on every task we needed to complete. They told you the way it was, without bullshitting or sugarcoating anything. If you couldn't grasp it or meet the standards put forward, pack your bags because you were leaving and going back to your unit without a Ranger Tab.

Lo and behold, within five minutes of our operations order (OPORD) class, everybody in our platoon was standing. Sleep deprivation was really starting to set in on all of us.

That evening was our final hand-to-hand session. It was four long, grueling hours of physical exhaustion. Throwing each other, punching one another, push-ups, flutter kicks, running around the pit, along with bear crawls and buddy carries until the early-morning hours. I was excited, though, because it being the last night of combatives training meant we were closer to getting through RAP Week and moving on to our first phase. Fifty-eight or fifty-seven days until graduation—I think. At this point, my classmates and I began to lose count. The days and nights were running together. "Just tell us the task we have to accomplish next in order to get to the next one after that" was the mentality.

Zero dark thirty the next morning started off with the two-mile buddy run in combat equipment, immediately followed by the infamous Malvesti Obstacle Course, also known as the "worm pit" obstacle course. It was called the "worm pit" because of the twenty-five-meter portion we had to crawl through with muddy water and knee-high barbed wire above our heads. I don't think I went through the run and obstacle course with Germany. I believe the RIs paired us up randomly with whoever was standing next to us before we were told to go at the beginning of the run. The run was conducted in BDUs, LCEs, boots, with rubber ducks. I cannot remember what the time standard was for the run, or if there even was one. Once complete, we lined up at the beginning of the course, grounded our weapons and LCEs, stayed with the same buddy and began negotiating the first obstacle. The worm pit resulted in a familiar outcome—an ass-smoking, drenched with muddy water, and cold because it was late September. After completing the obstacle course, we were told to move back to the barracks, shower, get into dry uniforms and look at the packing list for the next event, which was posted outside the headquarters.

That next event was a "fun-filled day" at the US Army Airborne School back on Main Post. After breakfast chow, we got on the buses for more singing and cheering from the Bat Boys. Hell, I was in such a good mood, I joined in the singing and grab-ass games too. Shit, we were about a day or two away from heading out to Darby Phase. The confidence was building up in all of us.

If you were Airborne qualified, you went through a day of Basic Airborne Refresher (where we were headed). First thing the next day, we would complete a jump in order to ensure that we were all current and qualified Airborne certified before we entered any of the Ranger School phases because there were parachute assaults integrated within the upcoming training. I remember feeling as though it was a waste of time for me since I was a current, qualified jumpmaster from the 82nd Airborne Division. However, I went through the classes and the training without saying a word, and did exactly what we were told. Too easy. I do remember I was made to exit the thirty-four-foot tower twice because the first time I exited I had my eyes closed—so the RI that was grading me said, "Unsatisfactory, Ranger, you had your eyes closed when you exited the paratroop door. Go back up the tower and exit again." My reply to him was "Roger that, Sergeant." I walked back up the steps of the tower and did it again with zero sarcasm or attitude. I knew how this "game" worked. If you expect to make it through these schools successfully, the number one thing you do not do is get into a pissing contest with those that evaluate and grade you.

We spent most of the day at Airborne School before heading back to Camp Rogers. Our jump time over Fryer Drop Zone the next morning was like 0800 or 0900. Once back at Rogers, we had extensive classes on demolitions, got to eat dinner chow at the mess hall, and then received more classes and hands-on training on communications and weapons disassembly and reassembly. After our Airborne operation in the morning, we were going to test on the M240B machine gun, the M249 squad automatic weapon (SAW), the AT-4 anti-tank weapon, the M-21A1 Claymore mine, filling out a range card on a machine gun position, and placing the SINGARS radio into operation. Almost sounded like a miniature Expert Infantryman Badge (EIB) testing. Sounded like it was going to be a relatively easy day. For once, no obstacle course, or long run, or hand-to-hand combat session.

That evening before we could bed down, all the Airborne-qualified students had to rig our rucks and M-1950 weapons cases to jump. We were each issued a rubber duck to place inside instead of real weapons. The RIs went through and inspected each to ensure that they were properly rigged. We then went through sustained Airborne training, or pre-jump, which is mandatory training prior to any jump. All this was put out of the way so that in the morning all we had to do was get on buses and head to the Departure Airfield on Main Post.

At zero dark thirty the next morning, we ate breakfast, got onto the buses with our rigged equipment, and headed to Main Post for our first jump in Ranger School. Once inside the pack-shed, we drew our parachutes and reserves and were told to start donning them and our equipment. We were jumpmaster personnel inspected (JMPI) by the RIs and took a seat on the benches, waiting for the next block of instruction. It was "nighty-night" time as we sat and waited to load the C-130 aircraft. There were two chalks, or two aircraft, that we finally loaded when the sun came up. There was no wasting time. Once loaded into our seats, the pilots took off and headed straight for the drop zone. The non-jumpers or non-Airborne students were on drop-zone details, to include parachute collection and part of the drop-zone safety teams. We all exited the aircraft with no issues; at least, I didn't have any. I had a great daytime jump, great sunny weather, no wind, and a soft landing. As a matter of fact, it was one of the easier mornings at Ranger School up to this point in RAP Week, which was almost over!

Back at Rogers, we proceeded with our weapons and communications hands-on testing. I remember running into two of the Benning RIs that I was classmates with during ANCOC, which seemed to be a year ago at this time. They were both sitting down as I rotated through each testing station.

"Hey, Ranger, how's it going for ya so far?"

I was surprised to run into them; I knew they were RIs, but didn't quite know what phase.

"Pretty good so far, Sergeants. Moving along day by day."

One of them replied to me with, "You know you're the only one left from the ANCOC class, right? So keep driving on, Ranger."

I said, "Thanks, Sergeant, I will."

The other RI gave me a "good luck" as I walked back to the next testing station. I remember feeling good after they gave me that few seconds of encouragement. After all, they knew what rank I was, and that I was older than most there as well. Honestly, my unit back at Fort Bragg was pretty strict on making it an expectation to be Ranger qualified in order to be a platoon sergeant or platoon leader. It made my decision to be there, twelve years into my career, that much easier.

After our testing was complete, we were filed into a set of bleachers and received a motivational briefing from the Ranger Training Brigade (RTB) commander and command sergeant major. They basically told us that it appeared those of us remaining, which was probably close to half of the approximate 200 that started five days ago, had successfully completed RAP Week. The last event would be the next evening, when we would conduct the final event to pass, which was the dreaded fifteen-mile foot march out to Camp Darby. I'm not going to sugarcoat it; they did not tell us anything we weren't already aware of. Receiving a motivational speech from the RTB leadership was mandatory, but we could have used that time to get more training on how to succeed in the upcoming initial phase.

That final evening at Camp Rogers was spent packing our rucksacks according to the Darby packing list. I must say, after the rucks were completely packed, they were pretty damn heavy. We also spent the time getting our equipment put together according to the Ranger School standard operating procedures (SOPs). For example, our two-quart canteens and entrenching tools attached to our rucksacks, ammunition pouches and other items attached to our LCEs, and every piece of equipment being tied off with 550 cord, secured with the "infamous" Ranger School in-line bowline knot.

The last day of RAP Week, we received extensive classes on tactical movement formations, using hand-and-arm signals. Also, moving into and setting up a security perimeter and objective rally point (ORP). These were just as much part of a graded patrol as the mission itself. Movement into an ORP during combat operations is a detailed, step-by-step process where the squad or platoon sets up their final security area before moving on to their mission. It's their final area where they finalize the plan, re-camouflage themselves and equipment, and ground their rucksacks and/or equipment not needed for the mission itself. The assault element moves out of the ORP through a release point, where each Ranger is counted out. A small element remains back and pulls security at the ORP and also monitors the element conducting the mission through radio communications. Before moving out, the leader getting ready to move out will leave the leader staying back with a five-point contingency plan. This explains where they are going, what mission they will be doing when they get there, the estimated time they will be gone on the mission, what they will do if they run into enemy contact on the way, and actions to take if the ORP security gets attacked by the enemy.

All this sounds relatively easy, and for the most part it is. Except in Ranger School, they take away two elements that would make this process much easier—food and sleep. We practiced these tasks all day before moving out to Camp Darby that early evening.

We cleaned the barracks that we spent very minimal time in during the past few days, and loaded our duffle bags inside a container that would be transported to Darby. Like I said earlier, we only had a little over 100 students remaining from zero day. Darby Phase recycled students would be integrated with our class once we organized squads after arriving to Camp Darby later that evening. We all drew actual weapons from the arms room (no more rubber ducks), to include machine guns and the tripods that go along with them. We were ordered to tie a piece of 550 cord from our weapons to our LCEs on our bodies. We were to never be caught by any instructor not having our weapons secured to our bodies at all times when moving on a tactical operation, from this point until the end of Ranger School. If you lost your weapon or any other sensitive item such as night vision, you would obviously and automatically be dropped from the course. So, having your weapon tied off to you was an insurance policy, especially under sleep deprivation.

We moved out right around dusk and headed out of Camp Rogers, on our way to Camp Darby. The standard was pretty simple— do not fall back too far, or fall out completely. If a student does, they will be dropped from the course, no retest on the foot march. The cover of the Ranger Handbook we were issued on zero day had printed on it in bold lettering, "Not for the weak or fainthearted." They weren't bullshitting.

It was a typical pace for a tactical road march. Two columns, one on each side of the road, staggered formation. We stepped it out with a good pace, but not an extreme fast pace. It was as comfortable as it could be, with a cool September evening. After a few hours of walking, we finally turned off the road and headed on a trail, which I had heard about from previous horror stories. It was a rocky, unending trail that led us uphill for at least a mile, right into Camp Darby. It was even darker out once we left the main road because the trail was in the thick, Georgia woods. I remember falling on the son of a bitch several times, and getting more pissed off every time I did. That's all you heard on the way up: "Fuck!" We were already exhausted from the march itself, and now we were tripping over rocks and tree roots embedded into the thin trail. "When the fuck is this trail gonna end!?" These were the shouts coming from the students. Then you would hear an RI shout out, "Shut the fuck up, Rangers. Quit the fucking crying and dry up your tears!"

We finally staggered into the camp like zombies. We formed up under a single light outside an old-looking Quonset hut and were told to stand by. I swear we must have been standing there forever. Nobody took off their rucks; we desperately wanted to but didn't dare because we weren't told to do so. Finally, after about a half hour or so, an RI came out of the hut.

"Rangers, when I call out your roster number, fall in to my right, your left, Rangers."

He was putting us in our assigned squads for Darby Phase. We did lose a few more on the foot march out, not quite sure how many. At this point, all I could think about was grounding my ruck and getting the fucking weight off my back. There was a formation of students off to the side that I assumed were the Darby recycles waiting for us to arrive. They too were integrated into the squads the instructor was forming.

After the squads were formed into thirteen-man elements, the RI sounded off with, "Alright, Rangers, RAP Week has officially ended, and Darby Phase begins now. Ground your rucksacks at your feet and stand by for your instructors. We're about to issue your squad equipment. Do not sit down, and God forbid you fall asleep, Rangers. Stay your asses awake. We're not in the business of feeling sorry for your asses out here, Rangers." Again, they were calm with hardly any yelling or screaming. It was their tone and seriousness that had you concerned—and some a bit scared. At approximately 0200 hours, we began Darby Phase of Ranger School.

CHAPTER 3

DARBY PHASE
SQUAD-LEVEL EVALUATIONS

The issuing of our squad equipment seemed like it took forever, probably because it did. I really don't remember everything they signed over to us, just that it was a shitload of stuff. One item that I do remember for sure was the medical kit bag. That thing was big and bulky. It was a cylinder-shaped canvas carrier—real nice when it rained and got wet and added another ten pounds to our already sixty to eighty-pound rucksacks. Inside were typical medical supplies, such as gauze, bandages, small bottles of bleach for purifying river and stream water we drank, and a litter system for carrying the wounded. I want to say we were even issued laminated maps of the areas where we would be conducting our upcoming operations.

Anyway, this particular initial equipment issue was a long, drawn-out process that took at least two hours, I would estimate. The RI issuing it to us kept going inside the cadre hut and leaving us out there to inventory the equipment with his sheet he gave us. We were exhausted from the march and lack of sleep from the past six days. One thing was for sure; we knew we weren't going to sleep anytime soon, and it was well after 0200 in the morning—hell, maybe even after 0300. I remember saying to myself, "Damn, this Ranger School sleep thing really does suck." In reality, the exhaustion and tiredness I felt that first night at Darby was nothing compared to what was to come.

"Alright, platoon leader, do your squad leaders have all their assigned equipment and has it been inventoried?"

"Yes, Sergeant."

"OK, PL, because you're signing my platoon hand receipt. Therefore, you had better check all your squads thoroughly, Ranger."

We all stood there in the dark and were like, "Sign the shit so we can move on to sleep." That didn't happen either. He signed for the equipment, and then we distributed it among ourselves as evenly as we could figure. The RI came out of the hut again and said, "OK, PL, you got it all packed up yet?"

"Not quite yet, Sergeant."

"Well, PL, when you 'quite yet' get it packed in your rucks, I'll take you down to your new Darby home for the next couple of days. I'll be back out and check on you all in a few minutes, or whenever you decide to un-fuck yourselves and get your equipment packed up, Rangers. We're on your time now." His "few minutes" meant about a half hour later.

We finally got our equipment packed up, and were standing around, falling asleep on our feet. He came back out and asked if everything was packed. "OK, Rangers, follow me."

We were under the impression that we were going to a barracks, like back on Camp Rogers. Those days were gone. Instead, we were taken to a pavilion area with a couple tables underneath the overhead cover. "This is your planning bay area, Rangers. Get some rest, and, PL, I want everybody back up, outside the cadre building in two hours. Y'all got the Darby Queen in a couple hours, Rangers, so get some rest."

He didn't have to tell any of us twice. I pulled my wooby out of my ruck, lay down in the grass and went to sleep. We were too tired to worry about being too sore from the foot march, ahead of negotiating the biggest obstacle course in Ranger School, which was apparently going to take place in the next couple of hours.

Two hours later we were woken up by our PL. I grabbed my personal hygiene kit out of my rucksack, brushed my teeth, quickly poured some water in my canteen cup, pulled out my little mirror, some soap, and a razor, and got to shaving—quickly. I put my hygiene kit back in my ruck, along with my wooby, put on and tied up my boots, and I was ready to go. Not really. I and everybody else were tired as hell and were in "zombie mode." Me and Germany walked towards the cadre shack, pulled out our one-quart canteens from our LCEs and filled them up from the water buffalo near our formation area. I looked at him and asked, "You ready for the Darby Queen, dude?"

"Hell no," he replied. Our feet were still chewed up from the foot march, but we were ready to get this over with. Now that it was daylight, I looked around this camp. It was old and gloomy looking. Seriously, this place looked as old as Ranger School itself. There were a few Quonset huts that were painted camouflage and some metal containers off to the left of our formation area. It was still kind of dark because this camp was in the middle of the Georgia woods. Small trails broke off and led down to each platoon's planning bay.

The RIs came out of the cadre hut and walked towards us. "PL, you got everyone? You up on all your weapons and equipment? Nobody quit last night, did they?"

The PL replied, "Yes on personnel and equipment, and no on anybody quitting last night, Sergeant." It is difficult to refer to the timeline of two and a half hours ago as "last night," but that was becoming the norm in this place.

"Alright, Rangers, I assume everybody has their canteens topped off, right? If not, there's a couple water buffalos on site, Rangers. Let's go; follow me." He led us down the hill on a firebreak that led out of the camp.

After about a twenty-minute walk, we were led into an open grassy area. "OK, Rangers, ground your weapons, LCEs, and patrol caps, and gather around this map board. Welcome to the Darby Queen Obstacle Course, Rangers! This will be your first graded evaluation here at

Darby Phase. If you do not negotiate an obstacle to standard, i.e., if you fall off or do not complete it in full, you will be given a second chance to complete it to standard. If you cannot, you will receive a minor-minus spot report, Rangers. If you choose to not attempt the obstacle at all or freeze up in the middle of negotiating the obstacle, you will receive a major-minus spot report, Rangers. Understood?"

We all replied, "Yes, Sergeant!"

"OK, Rangers, jog in place and remain moving at a double time throughout the entire course! First two Rangers, GO!"

So, before I go on any further, let me explain how the grading and evaluation factors work during each phase of Ranger School. Ways to recycle any of the three phases are as follow: Number one, if a student fails or No-Gos their graded patrol, they have to have a Go on the leadership position they are picked for. If there is time remaining in the phase, they may be afforded a second or even a third chance, depending on the size of the class. If it's a larger class that has to get graded on a leadership position, the student may only be afforded one chance for an evaluation. The patrols are broken down in two segments of grading within a twenty-four-hour period. The first half of the mission is the planning phase, and then a "change of mission" will be ordered, and the cadre will pick a new group of students to change leadership positions for the second portion, or the actions-on portion.

Number two, if a student receives three major-minus spot reports. If the student fails a mandatory test the first time, but gets a Go the second chance, he receives a major-minus. If he fails the test or task twice, he automatically goes to a board of decision-makers for that phase to recycle. The board usually includes a company or battalion-level commander. Also, a student caught sleeping during a mission where it may be a safety issue or hinder the mission itself could earn himself a major-minus. Usually, it's the RI's discretion. Three minor-minus spot reports equal one major-minus. Again, RI's discretion.

Lastly, if a student receives a low-rating peer evaluation at the end of each phase, they will more than likely get recycled in that phase. In other words, if your squad members do not think you're up to the job or not an asset to the squad, they may peer you last or towards the bottom of the list. Again, the cadre will also be observing conduct within the squads themselves. No student or squad as a whole will get anything over on any of the RIs. More details on this subject will come later on in my story of my experience in this school. Any student can recycle any of the phases as many times as it takes for them to pass and move on. During my time in the Army I'd known soldiers that spent six months to a year in Ranger School, prior to being there myself.

There are two ways of leaving Ranger School—actually three if you count successfully completing the course and graduating. One is voluntarily quitting, or what is known as LOM, lack of motivation. Any student can walk up to any cadre member and request to LOM anytime during the course. As a matter of fact, we already had plenty of them thus far. The second way to leave is receiving a serious observation report or SOR from any of the cadre. To earn an SOR, the student has a definite integrity violation, such as lying to the RI; becoming hostile with a cadre member or even a student; stealing from another student, to include food; and cheating or attempting to manipulate the system. Again, cadre's discretion. If a student has a negligent discharge with their weapon at any time during the course, they will be offered a "day-zero recycle." This means just that: In order to stay in Ranger School, you have to go all the way back to zero day and start all over with the Ranger PT test. I couldn't even imagine that, but it has happened, and it happened in my class at least one time.

Back to the Darby Queen. I started out moving up a hill, and when I began going over, it was a steep drop downhill. At the bottom of the hill was the first obstacle, which was the "belly-buster." A typical obstacle that is a familiar one at any course in the military. You have to jump up and on a log, and then up again and over a higher log.

When you come down, you are to land on your feet. Well, I landed on my back. I hit the obstacle with such momentum from running at it downhill that I went up and over and rolled right off the top log and came down about ten feet right on my back. I thought for sure the RI grading the obstacle was going to tell me to do it again.

Instead, he called me over and said to me with a smirk on his face, "Get the fuck out of here, old man, and good luck to you."

Lo and behold, it was another fellow ANCOC student who happened to be an RI at Fort Benning. "Thank you, Sergeant," I said as I ran to the next obstacle.

The Darby Queen Obstacle Course was the standard Army confidence course that is at Basic Training, Air Assault School, and most military installations. The difference here was that the obstacles were more spread out, making the student run up and down trails to get to them—a physical-fitness ass-smoking at each obstacle before you negotiated it.

I finished the course "almost successfully." I did earn myself a minor-minus spot report on one of the obstacles. It was an obstacle where you are to jump from tree stump to tree stump without touching the ground. I failed it twice and got a spot report. Honestly, I was glad it was over. My mentality was "Now let's get to patrolling, and get on with this phase." I moved back up the hill to my equipment, grabbed a canteen and slammed it down. My Ranger buddy, Germany, was already done with it too. He looked at me and asked, "Well, how'd you do?"

"I got a minor-minus, dude," I replied to him.

"Yeah, me too, man," he said.

"Which one?"

No shit, we both happened to get a spot report on the same damn, stupid little obstacle. We laughed and high-fived each other. "Too easy, brother!" The funny part was that we negotiated the high, difficult, even somewhat "scary" obstacles, but we couldn't get through this little one with one-foot-tall stumps. Give me a break!

"Way too fucking easy, dude. Darby Queen was like *George Washington*—history."

The next two days at Camp Darby were focused on cadre-led training and classes on planning and conducting a mission, down to the precise detail on how each squad-level combat operation would be graded for the next week and a half. The RIs set us up at each of the platoon's planning bays and went through extensive classes on how the planning phase should be conducted from beginning to end. Everything from the warning order (WARNO) and operations order, to the terrain-model briefing, to rehearsals on a tentative mission were explained to us. The OPORD was imbedded into our heads to the point where we simply had to fill in the blanks on the dry-erase boards or butcher-block paper when briefing our squads and fire teams. We did this well into the night and practiced missions until early the next morning. We stayed relatively close to the camp. The next day and night, we conducted a full planning phase, and an actions-on phase that was led by the RIs assigned to each thirteen-man squad. A Ranger squad consisted of the standard light-infantry squad, which was a squad leader, two fire team leaders, two riflemen, two automatic riflemen, two grenadiers, and a four-man machine-gun crew consisting of a gunner, assistant gunner, ammunition bearer, and an anti-tank gunner.

The typical squad missions in Darby primarily consisted of movement to contact, react to a near ambush, far ambush, react to indirect fire, and conducting a reconnaissance on an enemy site. There was nothing really "special" or out of the ordinary when it came to conducting these operations in Ranger School. It was typical Field Manual 7-8 standards. The main things we had to take with us and learn were the step-by-step processes required to meet RTB standard, especially in the planning phases. The three graded leadership positions in Darby were squad leader, and alpha and bravo team leaders.

On the third morning at Camp Darby, it was on; playtime was over. We began our first graded combat patrols in Ranger School.

We started at zero dark thirty, with our first mission. I truly cannot remember what type of mission it was, but it was a long and drawn-out twenty-four hours—all days were from here on out. We did about three or four days of graded patrols and then ended back at Camp Darby for a day of retraining on typical improvements that the cadre noticed on the patrols. This was a natural portion of the training calendar that was scheduled, and not an interruption of patrolling because we were "chewed-up" or anything like that. Ranger School is set up so that the three phases are based off of a "crawl, walk, run" concept. Our class was obviously in the crawl phase.

Germany and I had been placed into different squads, and he had already been graded on a mission, and was quite confident that he was a Go on it as well. I had yet to be called up for a leadership evaluation by this time. I remember asking Germany how it was being graded. He said it was just like going on a regular training mission, back at your home base, during a field exercise.

"Just treat it like that, don't think about being graded, and you'll have no problem." Then he finished it off with, "Too easy." He and I broke out an MRE (meal ready to eat) and devoured it as if it were our last meal and we were going to the electric chair the next day. I wished I could say "Too easy" along with my Ranger buddy, but I had yet to be graded at this point.

So, the RI grading you gives you a quick after-actions review (AAR) right after your mission, when the squad is usually back into the ORP or patrol base. They'll give you "sustains and improvements" that you as the student need to work on. You can get the vibe during the AAR whether or not you are a Go or No-Go. If you receive the majority of "sustains" over "improvements," you're more than likely a Go on your patrol. Technically, the RIs are not supposed to tell you whether you are a pass or fail until your final AAR when the phase is officially over—I say "technically."

Back out in the field, I finally heard my roster number called for a leadership position.

"Roster Number Five-Zero, Alpha team leader. Let's go, Rangers, get up here for your mission briefing." It was a movement to contact operation, and I was Alpha team leader for the planning phase and movement. You never know when your land navigation skills will be put to the test, and today was my time. I knew that the movement was going to be the main focus on my evaluation from the RI. Getting from point A to point B was going to be my main responsibility, along with security as the squad's point man, of course. Failure to stay on azimuth and keep a precise pace count would cost not only me a passing grade, but the student being evaluated as the squad leader as well. Once we were briefed by the RI, I said to myself, "OK, it's time to go to work." I began planning the route to the grid coordinate that we were to move to, which turned out to be a three or four-kilometer movement from where we were, deep inside the southern Georgia woods.

During the terrain-model briefing, I explained the route, the distance, the azimuth on our heading, and that I would be identifying en-route rally points along the way as per SOP. During the rehearsals portion, we covered hand-and-arm signals and movement techniques, such as moving in a wedge and file formation in accordance with the terrain. Since this was a movement to contact, we knew that enemy contact was probable, if not imminent, so we prepared for that and did a battle drill for reacting to contact. The planning phase seemed to be perfect and went off without a hitch. It was time to re-camo our faces and conduct final inspection checks on equipment, canteens full, etc. I had my Ranger beads ready to go, tied off to my suspenders of my LCE, and my compass was attached to one of my front breast pockets. The squad took a knee, and we were silent from here on out. All we could hear were the birds above us, and the crickets chirping in the thick wooded area. Everybody faced out for security. The Bravo team leader and one of the gun crew members came up to the front and were prepared to count us out of our security perimeter. One of the RIs gave the squad leader a thumbs-up to go ahead and take off. He gave me the hand-and-arm signal to move out.

My first graded patrol in Ranger School went pretty smooth, I must say. I stayed on my azimuth, had good confidence in my pace count, and kept my head on a swivel during the whole movement. We were quiet, slow moving, but not too slow either. Eventually we came out of the wooded area, and I saw an open area ahead of us that seemed to be a couple hundred meters long. I gave the signal for halt and took a knee. The squad leader came up and asked me what was up. I showed him the open area and told him to prepare either for small arms contact, indirect fire, or both. We knew better than to go off azimuth and attempt to go around the open area. Murphy's Law would have us getting too far off course, and then the next thing you know, we would end up getting lost. *Lost*—a dirty word in Ranger School that no student ever wants to use. Make no mistake about it, at this point we were going on several days in the field, and everybody was already in zombie mode. The squad leader told me to stay on course and pick up the pace across the open area, and that we would spread out the formation as well. I told him, "Roger that." All of a sudden, here he came, the RI. As a matter of fact, it was the RI that was grading me specifically.

He took a knee beside me and pulled out his map. "OK, Ranger, show me where you think we're at." I didn't even hesitate and pointed right to the edge of the open area.

"We're right here, Sergeant," I replied.

He then asked, "Where do you think your end point is, Ranger?" He didn't say "objective" because it was a movement to contact and not an assault, ambush, or recon, or even a link-up point.

I said to him, "It's approximately two hundred meters just past that wood line, beyond this open area, Sergeant." I always preferred the word *approximate* instead of *about* because it sounded like you were more certain about your decision.

"OK, Ranger, drive on." The RI then walked back to the rear of the formation. That meant that I was pretty much right on, because we'd already noticed that if you were off course, they would give little hints like, "You might want to do a map check, Ranger, or check your compass and azimuth, Ranger." When they told you to "drive on," and left you alone, that pretty much meant you were good. I got motivated really quick, and my confidence shot through the roof. I turned around and gave the squad leader a thumbs-up, and he gave me the signal to move out.

As soon as the whole squad was in the open, we heard the loud whistling sound of indirect fire. Everybody sounded off with "Incoming!" We all hit the ground, facedown, and waited to hear the explosion. The squad leader gave us a distance and direction, and everyone got up and double-timed to that area. We encountered one more explosion and repeated the drill until we were back inside the woods on the other side of the open area.

One thing happened to me that I still remember to this day. Once we got to the edge of the wood line, out of the open area, I fell right into a fucking hole, up to my waist.

"Fuck!" I shouted.

The squad leader and another student grabbed my arms and pulled me out. I needed help because I only had about seventy or eighty fucking pounds on my back. I didn't have time to dwell on it; I just got out and had to continue moving. Once deeper inside the woods again, we halted and took a knee to get a head count before continuing movement.

One of the RIs came up and said, "Alright, squad leader, change of mission." This meant our graded time was over and three different students would get called out for the leadership positions. The RI grading me came up and asked if I was all right or if I was injured. Apparently, he saw my fall into the hole back there. I think the hole was an old fighting position for training that was not buried completely because I saw a couple sandbags on the sides as they pulled me out.

"No, I'm good, Sergeant."

Anyway, we changed leadership positions and received a new mission that took us well into the hours of darkness. I never did receive that first short AAR from the RI, probably because the next day we were heading back to camp, to the end of the phase.

After our mission, we moved into a patrol base to link up with the other squads, so our whole platoon was together again. They never did change out leadership from the mission we just had. Instead, they kept it going throughout the whole night. They were still being graded on patrol base activities—poor bastards. Hell, I even went around the perimeter and checked on guys to ensure they were awake and even whispered that the same guys were still being graded. This was probably the hardest thing to do throughout Ranger School—to stay awake and active inside the patrol base at night, especially since everybody was "smoked." Oh yeah, the best part was that it had been raining on us for the past two hours straight.

As the sun was about to come up, I was wet and cold. The rain had stopped about an hour prior. I had the guy next to me cover down on security while I grabbed my ruck and fell back off of the perimeter a little to change into dry BDUs. I took my ziplock bag out of one of my breast pockets. Inside, I had a notepad, mechanical pencil, and most importantly, my military ID card. I set it on the ground and changed my clothes. Before moving back to the perimeter, I forgot one thing—to put my ziplock bag into the dry uniform I had on. Instead, I left it lying there on the ground, like a freaking dumbass.

"Alright, Rangers, change of mission! Secure your equipment! PL, once you got accountability of personnel and equipment, there's a firebreak over there. Get the platoon on it and we'll move you back to camp, Ranger. Roger that?"

"Hooah, Sergeant," the platoon leader replied. We got on the firebreak and foot-marched about a mile back to Camp Darby. It wasn't until we got back to camp that I discovered I had left my ID card back at the patrol base. I didn't dare say anything. Again, you never say the words *lost* or *misplaced* in Ranger School. I knew that we were going to get an eight-hour refit break once we got back to Camp Rogers. I'd worry about a new ID card then, but for now, I was waiting to get my final-phase AAR from the Ranger instructor that graded me.

As soon as we arrived at Camp Darby, the RIs wasted no time and sat us down in formation to begin our peer evaluations on one another within our squads. You went down the list of names and roster numbers and numbered each from one to thirteen or however many students you had in the squad. It was pretty quick and painless.

About a half hour later, the RIs started giving each student their final AARs for the entire phase. "Roster Number Five-Zero!"

"Yes, Sergeant!"

"Let's go." He was sitting on a tree stump with a little stack of manila folders beside him. One of them had my roster number on it, and inside, I'm assuming, were my records during the course thus far. I stood in front of him at the position of parade rest. He started right off with the patrol I was graded on. He gave me "sustains" on my movement, land navigation skills, security, leadership, and technical and tactical proficiency. He gave me an "improve" on situational awareness because I had fallen into that hole. I simply said, "Roger that, Sergeant." He then told me that I was an overall Go on my graded patrol.

He went over the other requirements to be able to move on, which were negative spot reports and peer evaluations. I had the one minor-minus spot report from the Darby Queen, and had a pretty good peer evaluation of 80 percent or higher. I then heard the words I had been waiting for: "You are being recommended to move on to the Mountain Phase of Ranger School, Roster Number Five-Zero. Any questions for me, Ranger?"

"No, Sergeant," I replied.

"OK, move out."

I got back to the formation area and found Germany. He looked at me and asked, "So?"

I gave him the famous answer, "Too easy."

He looked at me and said, "Oh, entirely too fucking easy."

The trucks pulled up, we loaded them, and we headed out of Camp Darby for the rest of our lives; well, most of us did. Others unfortunately were getting recycled and would have to stay there and start the phase all over again when the next class came staggering in from their fifteen-mile foot march.

Back at Camp Rogers, we unloaded our duffle bags and formed up for a briefing from the RIs.

"OK, Rangers, you're getting eight hours of mandatory refit time. A bus will be taking you to Main Post, to the big shoppette area. Once there, you can take a taxi anywhere on Main Post if you want to go anywhere else. Do not go off post, Rangers! I know y'all are gonna just worry about food, Rangers; we've been in your boots once before too! I suggest besides Burger King and Popeye's Chicken, y'all get your nasty uniforms washed at the laundromat. Get to the shoppette and buy yourselves items you may need, such as 550 cord, new socks, T-shirts, personal hygiene items, or whatever.

"Don't waste this eight hours, Rangers! Once I release you, go take a shower and get your nasty asses cleaned up, and put on your civilian clothes you brought. The bus will leave in about an hour. It will pick you up at the same spot it drops y'all off on Main Post at 1600. Be safe, Rangers, and don't get into trouble out there! Dismissed!" We all cheered and clapped.

On the bus, I told my Ranger buddy about what happened to my ID card, and that I would have to go get a new one before I did anything else. I knew where we were getting dropped off, and I knew where the ID card facility was from there too. It was all in walking distance. We got dropped off, and I took my dirty clothes straight to the laundromat, which was right there in the shopping center area. After I got the washer going, me and Germany went over to the ID card place. I told him he didn't have to go with me because, shit, I knew he was as hungry as I was.

"Man, go get some food, dude. I'll take care of my ID card and catch back up to you in a few."

"Nope, we're in this shit together, brother."

I was like, "OK, let's get this bullshit done."

It was a painless process. Hell, I just made it through the first phase of Ranger School. What could I complain about? It took about a half hour to get my new ID, and it was off to Burger King from there. One thing I wished I had worn with these jeans I was wearing—a fucking belt! My pants were a thirty-three-inch waist, and I was walking around holding them up with one hand like a fool. I had lost that much weight in the last sixteen days or so. Who cares, right? I was about to eat a double whopper, large fries, and a large Coke. What the hell, let's throw in a side of chicken nuggets with it too. Something else we didn't realize: our stomachs were smaller, too, so we got full much quicker. Plus, we ate as if the world were ending that day.

After our clothes were clean, we took a cab back to Camp Rogers early. We weren't going to wait until 1600. Once we got back, I shaved my head in the latrine back in our barracks, put on a clean pair of BDUs, put the other clean uniforms back into my duffle bags, and went nighty-night, until it was time for formation later. Man, I was going to get about four straight hours of sleep—the most I'd had at one time since I'd been there.

After formation that early evening, our class received another surprise. I'd heard rumors, but didn't know if it was true or not. We got a grilled hot dog meal, provided by the Benning RIs. It was fricking awesome. It was a tradition in Ranger School. Each student paid like five dollars for a hot dog, a bag of chips, a soda, and a candy bar. We thought we had died and gone to heaven. A Burger King meal for breakfast/lunch and hot dogs for dinner! I must say, the Ranger instructors were pretty decent human beings and a bunch of great guys. We sat around and laughed and told stories about the Army and Darby Phase as we ate our chow on a back-patio area over by the

Camp Rogers chow hall. The Benning RIs really let us be carefree for that evening before we left to go up north. However, I would soon find out in the upcoming phase that there was a small percentage of bad instructors at Ranger School, just as there is in any other military training environment. I was a drill sergeant for two years about a year prior to being there, and we had "shit-bag" instructors there as well. I used to see it firsthand, and it really tested my patience.

The next morning at zero dark thirty, we cleaned the barracks, formed up with all our equipment, and got on the buses. We were headed on a four-hour drive up north to Dahlonega, Georgia, which was a small community in the Appalachian Mountains. It was the end of September and starting to get a little chilly outside. The Bat Boys were in full effect again, back with the singing and loud laughing, and grab-ass games. Those kids were sure full of energy. Again, you would have thought that they had just come back from a vacation or some shit instead of just completing a phase of Ranger School.

CHAPTER 4

CAMP MERRILL:
SLING ROPES, STEEL OVALS,
& BLUEBERRY PANCAKES

When we arrived at Camp Merrill, I got off the bus and was amazed at how beautiful the scenery surrounding the camp was. It was the first time I had ever seen this portion of the United States. Everything was so green, with the mountains and hills in the background. All the roads and buildings on Merrill seemed to be built into the hills. The closest I'd come to this type of scenery was when I was stationed at Fort Lewis, Washington.

Then reality set in. I quickly realized that, very soon, I would be humping up and down these hills while carrying heavy weight on my back. I shook my head and grabbed my bags and ruck from the bottom compartments of the bus.

About 100 of us came up from Benning. We lost count of how many were left from the original class on day zero because of those that were dropped, quit, or recycled. There were another eighty or so Mountain recycles waiting to integrate with us. So, we were back at two companies of trainees with the capacity of two full platoons each going into the phase.

The RIs came out and told us to form up in the platoons we were already assigned to from Benning. It started raining, so they

NATHAN AGUINAGA   45

gave us our barracks right off the bat and told the PLs to get us up there to ground our gear on a bunk and to hurry and get back down to formation. We got inside the barracks, and it was different from Camp Rogers. It appeared to be an updated-style barracks, with two or three stories, open bays with latrines at the ends of them. If I'm not mistaken, the bunks weren't set up as double bunks, either. They were set up as single beds. Me and Germany found two bunks next to each other, threw our shit on them, and got back downstairs to formation.

We marched over to the 5th Ranger Training Battalion headquarters, and were told to take a seat across the street in a little open area, and to stand by for the battalion commander and command sergeant major's briefing. I can still see Camp Merrill as if it were yesterday.

I failed to mention earlier that each phase of Ranger School was run by 4th, 5th, and 6th Ranger Training Battalions, 4th being Benning, 5th at Mountains, and 6th was Florida. They all fell under Ranger Training Brigade Command at Fort Benning.

The battalion commander came out and gave us his pep speech, which was pretty down to earth, with no bullshitting us students.

"On behalf of myself and the command sergeant major, we would like to welcome each of you to Camp Merrill, Georgia, Rangers! Congratulations, first of all, on your successful completion of the Darby Phase of Ranger School. As you know, you will be upgraded to more responsibility during your time here at 5th RTB, where you will move from squad to platoon-size operations. As I'm sure you already are aware of, Rangers, Mountain Phase is where most students will recycle, and/or will be dropped from the course, either voluntarily or forced out for some kind of violation of integrity. Reason being, you're going to receive less sleep, food, and the terrain is going to kick most of your asses, Rangers. Some of you to your breaking points, Rangers. Listen to your instructors, follow their lead, always do the right thing, even if it's maybe the hard way, follow the tactical standards of FM 7-8 and your Ranger

Handbooks, and you will have no problem making it out of here successfully, Rangers!"

The RIs stepped back in front of us, and one of them explained the timeline of the Mountain Phase. "Today, Rangers, we're going to focus on getting you all in-processed into 5th RTB, starting with a thorough medical check by our medics, and then move over to your companies to ensure your packets are up to date and ready for evaluations. This next week will be focused on lower and upper basic mountaineering techniques. You will receive your lowers here at Camp Merrill, and then we will march up to Mt. Yonah for uppers training and testing, Rangers. So, we don't want you worrying about combat operations right now; you need to focus on mountaineering first, Rangers. One step at a time!"

Once we marched over to the medical station, we filed in when our roster numbers were called off, and each of us were personally checked by an Army medic from head to toe with a thorough screening. "Take off your boots, socks, and pull up your pant legs." They really paid close attention to your feet, ankles, shins, and knees. The medic went up feeling both my legs, up to my knees, and then squeezed on both of them.

"Owww," I said in a low tone—ensuring I did not yell or draw attention to myself.

"You have cellulitis in both knees," the medic said to me.

My heart immediately sank. "What does that mean? Does that mean I have to recycle or get hospitalized?" I caught myself going into panic mode. All I could think about was getting medically recycled or, even worse, medically dropped from the course.

He reassured me, "No, don't worry about it; it's in the beginning stages. I'm going to prescribe you an antibiotic that you'll take once a day for about the next ten days and you should be good. You'll be able to continue on." I was so relieved to hear this.

Well, it was happening; my body was being affected by this school. We weren't just losing weight quickly; we were getting skin bacteria, too. Camp Darby really put more of a hurting on me than I thought. *Oh well, suck it up and drive on.* I was happy to be able to keep going uninterrupted.

The medic then took out a needle and began pushing it into spots on my feet, and then squeezing out the puss. Apparently, I had blisters that were so thick I didn't even realize that they were blisters. I thought they were calluses forming, but the medic told me they were big blisters. So be it. "Fix me" was my mentality. I swear, going into that medical station was like taking your truck into Valvoline for maintenance so that you can get it back on the road for another three or five thousand miles. It was like a one-stop-shop because when he was done examining me, he walked over, told the other medic behind a counter the prescription, and he handed me a small bottle with ten pills of antibiotics. I was then sent on my way. Too easy.

After our group was done with the medical screenings, they moved us over to our company headquarters for our records check and any more in-processing that we needed to complete for 5th RTB. We stood in formation in front of the small headquarters building, and off to the left of us was the rope corral. The corral was an area roped off by one main rope, with smaller pieces of rope, or sling ropes, draped over all around it for knot-tying practice and testing.

Before I continue any further with my Camp Merrill experience, I have to share a quick story of something I experienced before being in Ranger School. Almost exactly three years prior, I started Drill Sergeant School at Fort Jackson, South Carolina. During the initial week of school there, we had a student that absolutely did not have any interest in being there or being a drill sergeant period. At the time, he was a newly promoted sergeant first class and was assigned to Fort Bragg, as I was at the time. As a matter of fact, we were assigned to the same regiment of the 82nd Airborne Division, just in different battalions, so he and I quickly became acquaintances there.

He used to complain to me about not wanting to be a drill sergeant because he needed to start and complete his two years of rifle platoon sergeant time, and that this upcoming assignment would hinder that opportunity for him, hence hurting his career progression—so he thought. I mean, that's all this guy did every time I got around him was bitch about being there and try to figure how to get out of the assignment. I remember telling him that it was going to be virtually impossible to convince the Army that he needed to stay at Fort Bragg. Hell, he was already signed in and had begun the Drill Sergeant Academy. How he thought he was going to get out of it was beyond me, but I didn't pay too much attention.

He had been talking to the instructors at the school for a couple of days, and eventually, they took him to see the commandant so that he could express his noninterest in being there. Pretty much all the candidates had a noninterest in being in Drill Sergeant School. So after the commandant of the academy turned his request down, the senior drill sergeant instructor pretty much told him that if he failed the first written exam, which we were going to take in the next day or so, that he would be released from the school and sent back to his unit. He did just that and was sent home.

I remember that he was so excited to be leaving and going back to Bragg that he had seemed like a totally different person. I wished him luck, and he left the Drill Sergeant Academy. Well, lo and behold, it was still a military leadership academy, and he would be receiving a DA Form 1059 when he left. A 1059 is an evaluation form when any servicemember attends a leadership academy in the Army. It is placed in your official records along with your evaluation reports, which is pretty much vital for promotion and career progression. His 1059 was not good. It actually read that he was an academic-failure release from a leadership academy.

I heard that when he got back to the regiment at Fort Bragg, the brigade command sergeant major not only refused to send him back to a line company to become a platoon sergeant, but also made sure he got reassigned to some other unit outside the 82nd Airborne Division. I'm not quite sure where I heard this, but that was the word back in our unit when I came home on weekend pass from Fort Jackson. Yeah, he wanted out of the drill sergeant assignment so bad that he had overlooked the possibility of receiving a negative evaluation report for doing so, and he paid the price for it when he got back to Bragg. Virtually not only not being afforded the opportunity to become a platoon sergeant, but also pretty much stopping any further career progression from there on out. In other words, he would probably never make it past the rank of sergeant first class. Now, if memory serves me correctly, one of his arguments for not being at Drill Sergeant School was that he had already been an RI previously before going to Bragg, and that he had already had three years or so of "instructor time" for the Army.

Now, fast-forward three years later, at Camp Merrill, standing in formation outside of our company headquarters. Here he came walking out of the building and heading towards our formation. He was a tall, lanky man, with a cocky look to him, especially in his eyes. He was wearing civilian shorts and a T-shirt with flip-flops on, and an old, worn-out John Deere hat. He appeared as if he had just woken up after his previous shift or something, because he was not in the best of moods. He had a big old dip of snuff in his mouth and a Styrofoam cup that he was spitting in.

As he approached our formation, I said to him, "Hey, Sergeant, I remember you. What a small Army it is."

I think that was a mistake that I would come to regret in the next few days because he walked up to me and glared at me as if he was trying to remember who I was. He spit in his cup loud and with a purpose, and just shook his head and walked away from me. I think he had figured out who I was, which wasn't a bad thing in my mind at the time. Although I had absolutely nothing to do with him quitting Drill Sergeant School three years prior, I think he looked at me as part of a bad experience he had in the Army, not really too long ago. *Oh well*, I said to myself. I remember having an "it is what it is" attitude about him at first. Within the next few days, however,

I quickly realized he wasn't really feeling me being there or being in his presence at all.

After in-processing our records, we were told to file off and cover down on a sling rope inside the corral. "Does everyone have a sling rope in front of them, Rangers? Go ahead and secure the rope and make your way back to formation." They had us sign for the sling ropes and then two steel carabiners, or what most grunts refer to as "D-rings." They then told us to go up to the barracks and secure our helmets, LCEs and rucksacks, and be back downstairs in formation quickly. We had to strip the camouflage covers off our helmets and put a piece of masking tape in front and back of it with our roster numbers on them. Our other equipment was checked for proper configuration and tie-downs. We then went right into training for upcoming mountaineering techniques, starting with knot tying. We sat in that corral practicing several different kinds of knots well into the night.

They marched us over to eat dinner chow at our new chow hall, with the same procedures as Camp Rogers. Six students went out front of the formation, and we sounded off with the Ranger Creed, knocked out our six pull-ups, and moved right into the chow line to get our food. I noticed by this time six pull-ups were almost impossible, at least for me, so I busted out as many as I could on my own and then had the guy behind me grab my ankles and assist me for the one or two I needed to finish in order to complete six. I wasn't alone on this physical difficulty, either. Our bodies were definitely losing strength as the days rolled on in this environment. Afterwards, it was back in the rope corral tying knots under the lights until late into the darkness. Eventually, it was time to get to the barracks and sleep, with a little bit of fire guard in between.

The next morning in formation, the RIs had the recycles integrate into our two companies prior to reentering the chow hall for breakfast. All the rumors and urban legends of pancakes were real! Blueberry pancakes! Thick pancakes, too! I couldn't believe we were allowed to eat this. We were also fed eggs, bacon, sausage, you name it. I thought this was some kind of trick or something. Nope, "eat what you get" was the game plan. In reality, they were trying to get us fed for what was to come in the near future—a straight ten-day field exercise with minimal calories, hardly any sleep, and walking and maneuvering through terrain that is almost indescribable.

After chow, it was back at the rope-tying corral. "Alright, Rangers, who thinks they're ready to be graded on their knot tying?"

Germany and I raised our hands, along with pretty much the rest of our platoon. I think we had to randomly tie two or three knots at the RI's discretion. He called out the specific knot, and we would then tie it to the rope on the corral with our issued sling rope. It was quick and painless, and an easy Go. We formed back up, secured our rucks and moved in a file down a flight of stairs that were steep and long. The stairs ended and the path turned into a thin trail down the remainder of the high ground we were on, to an open valley area with trees and plenty of shade. It was the area of all "lowers" training activities. The area where we ended up, in the shade, was all about tying-techniques training and rappel preparations. To our right was an open area where the rappelling took place.

We started right off with the basic rappel-seat configuration class on tying our sling rope into a standard "Swiss seat" around our waist. Once everyone in the platoon had that figured out pretty precisely, we moved into the proper configuration of a belay harness, with a figure-eight knot. We did these two configurations consistently to the point where we could do it in our sleep. The RIs, like they were during Darby, were pretty laid-back and precise on teaching us how to properly accomplish the task at hand. They were very professional and did all they could to ensure that everybody understood the "how-to" on rope tying and configuring the rappel seat and belay procedures. Obviously, before we could move over to the rappel station at the fifty-foot rock cliff, we had to certify on these two tasks.

Here he came, the Drill Sergeant School RI. From here on out, I'll simply refer to him as "DSS." My Swiss seat was already a Go, graded by another RI. Now we had to rig up our belay harness with the figure-eight knot. Now, if my memory serves me (since it's been almost twenty years), we had to tie the belay rig with a figure-eight knot with the open loop on the end. The final pass-or-fail test on it was that when the loop was raised, if it went past your chin, then it was too long and a failing grade was given to the student. Anyway, DSS stopped in front of me as he was walking through the area grading us. He looked at me with a sinister expression.

"You ready for inspection, Ranger?"

"Yes, Sergeant," I confidently responded. He held and turned the rope in his hand as he inspected the knot. He then reached down and lifted vigorously on it, hard enough so that when he brought the loop up, it surpassed my chin. "Oh no, your belay rig is too long, Ranger. That's too bad. You are a 'No-Go' at this station."

He then pulled out a pad of blank spot reports and filled one out. I received my first major-minus spot report in Ranger School.

"Here you go, Ranger. I suggest you continue to train on the belay rig before you retest on this task. If you fail again, it will be an automatic board review to recycle this phase, Ranger."

As if I didn't already know this. I bit my tongue as hard as I could so that I did not mouth off to him. Now, I'm not that guy who's ever made excuses on my downfalls or failures, but this guy, no shit, was bound and determined to fail me on purpose, and he did. Why? Because I knew he had quit a school a few years back? Who the fuck cares? Apparently, he did, and had a chip on his shoulder for it, too. Oh yeah, there are real assholes in the Army.

As in any other training environment, a retest meant having a different instructor grading you. I received a Go for my retest on the belay. However, it still stuck in my mind for the rest of that day, that I had a major-minus looming over me this early in the game. We still had rappels, rock climbing, and one of the roughest field problems in Ranger School to be graded on before we could even think about moving on to the next phase. One event, one day at a time is what I kept telling myself.

We did the rappels off the small cliff at lowers to certify in order to move on to uppers certifications on Mount Yonah. We did both a "Hollywood" rappel and a combat equipment rappel to be able to move on. Hollywood is military slang for conducting either a rappel or parachute jump in just your helmet; no combat equipment, such as rucksack, LCE, or weapon. Too easy! The next morning was more blueberry pancakes and then over to the arms room to draw weapons. The RIs put us on LMTVs (Army five-ton trucks) with all of our gear, and off to Mount Yonah for the next day and a half we went.

It was about a half-hour to forty-five-minute ride on the back of the truck. When we got to the base of the mountain, we unloaded, threw our rucks on our backs, and up we went. The Ranger School tradition is foot-marching up Mount Yonah. As a matter of fact, a two-mile fast-paced foot march up the motherfucker.

"Let's go, Rangers, move your asses!"

I'd moved at high-speed paces on road marches in my day, but this shit was ridiculous! We hauled ass up the mountain—again, didn't seem like we were ever going to get there, but we eventually made it.

Once at the top, we marched into a small bivouac site and broke off into platoon formations. We grounded our gear and walked to the water buffalo to fill up our canteens. I admit, I was a little spent from that two-mile uphill hike. I slammed a canteen of water and filled it up again. Hydration was the key to success in Ranger School, especially in the final two weeks of Mountain Phase.

We walked down to the areas where we would be conducting our upcoming climbs and rappels. The RIs gave us some demonstrations and little tips on dos and don'ts for the next day's training and testing. They explained to us that tomorrow was going to consist of a half day doing climbing techniques, and the second half focusing on rappels. I remember standing on top of the area overlooking the view. I swear you could see the entire state of Georgia from up there. The worst part was actually looking down in front of us, at the cliffs we would be rappelling off of.

Germany looked at me and shook his head. "I don't know, man; this shit looks pretty high up and steep, dude."

I replied with a "No shit, I don't know about this shit." I then told him that we shouldn't worry, that we would get through it like everything else up to this point.

When we got back to our bivouac site, we were allowed to break out an MRE and eat it at our leisure as if it were a dinner at a five-star restaurant. We all sat in our platoon area, shooting the shit and enjoying our MREs. Then you heard the famous "MRE trade game" with the food. "Who wants a cookie bar for cheese spread?" "Right here! Right here!" "Who's got a peanut butter for cheese?" "Who wants a beef stew main meal for a chicken and rice?"

This went on the whole time we were breaking out our chow from our rucks. As a matter of fact, this trade game was the norm every time we had an opportunity to eat in a group like this in the field.

"Who wants my entire MRE? I'm not that hungry."

"Oh shit, right here, right here, man."

The response was, "Fuck you, I was just bullshitting, dude."

"No shit, who the fuck isn't hungry these days? I can't believe you fell for that shit!"

Everybody in the platoon just laughed. It was the best comradery experience you could ever have in Ranger School.

After dinner, the RIs wanted us to put on a little show for them. It was the opportunity for the students to put on skits to make fun of and/or imitate whatever and whomever. Imitate the RIs, each other, or the school itself. They gave us a heads-up, like about a half hour, for some of the students to put together a skit. It was something you commonly saw in basic training after two months with the same platoons and drill sergeants, not after about a month in Ranger School. I remember asking myself why they would have us do skits after about three days with these instructors, before we even had an opportunity to know them yet.

DSS was running the whole show. You could tell he was one of the senior RIs of 5th RTB, and he should be. After all, this was apparently his second time as a Mountain Phase RI in his Army career. Who the fuck does two Ranger instructor assignments, especially in the same place, doing the same job? Apparently, someone whose career was pretty much wrapped up and who probably wanted to retire from the Army at Dahlonega, Georgia. After all, it was a beautiful, scenic area of the country.

These were the thoughts running through my head as I sat there looking at him, while he laughed and joked with a big dip of chew in his mouth. At this point, he wasn't my favorite person in the world, as I'm sure I obviously wasn't his.

So, the skit show went on, and it was minimal. The Bat Boys led the way in putting on the entertainment for the RIs. They actually did some pretty good skits and impressions, almost to the point of insult. That's what was funny with these kids; they didn't seem to give a shit about any of the pressures of Ranger School. Most of them just went by day to day, laughing off most of the events, and going through carefree. Like I said earlier, most of us older guys were entertained by the fact that the Bat Boys seemed to be treating Ranger School like it was a vacation away from their units back home.

The instructors split us up the next morning. One company of trainees went to the rappel side, and the other remained at the rock-climbing portion. Our company's first half of the day was spent conducting the rock-climbing training and eventually the climbing tests. Several lanes were marked off by numbers to do the testing. One Ranger student would do the climbing, and one would assist him with the belay. Each lane was approximately a thirty-five to forty-foot climb. Some appeared to be more difficult than others, but at the end of the day, having to go through it twice, I believe they were about the same. That's right, I failed my first rock-climb test of Mountain Phase. The RI claimed that I used my knees one too many times during my tested climb. You are only allowed to use your hands and feet to do the climbs. No other portion of your body can touch the rocks at all. The RIs would usually give you one or two warnings to "watch the knees." Of course, guess who I had grading me on my first climb? DSS himself. It was my never-ending luck during my time in the mountaineering portion.

"Stop! Come on down, Roster Number Five-Zero." He ordered me to come down after I was damn near to the top of my climb. I'm not shitting; I was literally about two feet from completing my climb. "Roster Number Five-Zero, you failed to properly negotiate this climb due to unauthorized usage of your legs—primarily using your knees, Ranger. You are a No-Go at this station. Initial here, Ranger."

I had just initialed my second major-minus spot report in Mountain Phase of Ranger School. One more and I would automatically have to go before the board at the end of the phase for, more than likely, a recycle determination. Now I was nervous that I would either fail the second climb, or get another No-Go on one of the rappel tests coming up next. As the moments ticked by, I continued to mind-fuck myself. I believe that was DSS's goal too. I wasn't feeling paranoid anymore with this guy. I was now thoroughly convinced he was out to fuck me on this phase. Again, the only benefit at this point was that I would be using a different lane, with a different RI for my retest on climbing.

Just like the belay retest a couple days prior, I received a Go on my second climb. What was funny about it was that I climbed it in the same exact fashion as I did before—hands and feet, with hardly any contact between my knees and the rocks. Oh well, it was in the past, right? Yes, it was indeed! But I kept asking myself, *Am I going to get this asshole again during one of my upcoming rappel tests?* Probably, because that seemed to be the pattern thus far with this guy. Anyway, I didn't have time to dwell on it; I had to suck it up and drive on. Concentrate on the next task at hand. "That's how you're going to make it out of here, Nate," I told myself.

That afternoon, we moved over to the rappel lanes. The first one that I got tested on was a Hollywood rappel. The scenery was intimidating to look at. We were pretty high up there on Mount Yonah, looking across the landscape of northern Georgia. The rappel went down an approximately seventy-foot cliff. About halfway down, the standard was to let go of your rope, lean back and get into a spread-eagle position. The point was to have total confidence in your belay man. It was the same standard as any other confidence-building test. If the student shows fear or reluctance to let go of the rope and lean back, they will be a failure at the task.

"Let go of the rope, Ranger!" This was being shouted from the RI at the top of the cliff and also the one at the bottom monitoring the belay man's actions.

"Ranger, if you reach for the rope again without being instructed to do so, you'll be a No-Go. We will tell you when to grab the rope again. OK, grab the rope, and continue with the remainder of the rappel, Ranger." These warnings echoed across the test site.

The second graded rappel was on the other side of the mountain, in more of a wooded portion. It was in full combat equipment, with LCE, weapon, and our rucksack with some weight in it, but not Ranger School combat operations' seventy to eighty pounds of weight. About halfway down the cliff, there was an open area with no rock at our feet, so it was a free-style rappel for the second half of it. I received a Go on both rappels, and so did my Ranger buddy. We sat there sipping water from our canteens, happy that we were done with the first portion of Mountain Phase. For me, it came at a difficult cost of two major-minus spot reports, but it was time to move on and put it behind me. Thank God that DSS was not assigned to our company or platoon for the upcoming field-exercise grading. I believe he was assigned to the other, or maybe he was so senior that he was only assigned to the mountaineering portion of

5th RTB, if such a situation existed. Either way, I never saw my "old friend" DSS ever again.

The next three days back at Camp Merrill was nonstop tactical training, all at platoon level. We covered everything from writing and issuing platoon-level combat orders, to calling for fire, to medic training and calling in a nine-line MEDEVAC, setting up and conducting machine-gun drills, and of course, platoon-level battle drills and patrol techniques—primarily platoon attack or raid, ambush, and conducting a reconnaissance or "recon." We worked on our own internal platoon SOPs, such as our radio call signs, employment of our prisoner search, and aid and litter teams as well. This went on for three days straight, both day and night. By the time we were scheduled to move out for our upcoming ten-day field exercise, we were ready. The instructors even had a few hours set aside for tactical loading and unloading procedures of both the UH-60 Blackhawk and CH-47 Chinook helicopters.

Of course, we had a little time here and there for fun during our MRE mealtimes at our planning bay. It was similar to the planning bays at Darby, an open wooden structure with metal roofing. Inside was a couple butcher-block stands and a large sand table to construct a standard terrain model. Of course, once out in the field, the terrain models were never as detailed as they were back at the camp's planning bays. As a platoon, we had a pretty extensive terrain-model kit that was broken down in several ziplock bags and distributed among the squads. So, at any given time, any squad could break one out, and the leadership chosen could immediately begin constructing a terrain model. You had to have that shit ready to go, especially when you were out there for days, walking around like a zombie, hungry and tired, and not thinking so sharply.

"Who's got a cheese spread for a peanut butter packet?"

"Oh shit, right here, right here, man!"

"Who wants a pork patty for a beef stew?"

"Over here, man!"

"Who doesn't want their hot sauce?"

"Who wants a lemon pound cake?"

"Oh fuck! Right here, man, right here!"

"I got a cake for you; why don't you 'pound' it up your fuckin' ass?"

The whole platoon laughed and giggled. MRE time, for a short period, was our sanctuary away from the stresses of Ranger School. It was awesome. The comradery was tight among us. One unwritten rule in the military: if you want to bring any team together as a family, put them in a world of hurt together.

"Roster Number So-and-So!" an RI hollered out for my Ranger buddy, Germany.

"Yes, Sergeant!" he shouted back.

"Let's go. You got an emergency phone call from your unit, Ranger."

I remember thinking, *Man, this can't be good when you get called and interrupted out in the woods in Ranger School.* Something very serious had to have happened back home or at his duty station in Germany.

He was gone on the phone for about a half an hour. When he came back to the planning bay area, he and I walked off a little ways into the woods so that he could tell me what had happened. His six-year-old little girl had gotten hit by a car in the housing area he and his wife lived in. She had several broken bones and was in the hospital recovering. She was going to be fine and was going to heal back to 100 percent.

As he was telling me what happened, tears swelled in his eyes, and within seconds, he broke down crying. I put my arm around his shoulders and consoled him that his daughter was going to be fine and that she was safe and recovering. It didn't seem to help him because he insisted that he had to leave Ranger School and go back to Germany to be by her side. Now, as a father myself with two young toddlers at home, I felt his pain, and anger as well. Anger at the person that was speeding through the housing area and hit his little girl.

I had to ask him if his wife, who had called, told him he needed to come home and be with them. He had said no, that he just felt it was the right thing to do. That if he stayed in school, it might look selfish. I had to give him a reality check really quick because he was very serious about walking over to the RI and saying the three dreaded letters to him—LOM.

"Hey, man, what are you saying?" I asked him. "You're not seriously thinking about leaving, are you? Hey, man, she's going to be alright and she's going to recover just fine. You leaving and going back to her now will not change what happened. Instead, she will continue to recover like she is going to under professional medical supervision anyway, and you will be going back to your unit as somebody who quit Ranger School. You know you're in a long-range surveillance unit, which means if you quit this course, you'll have to leave and go into one of the mechanized infantry units down the street." I had to break it down to him in the details of the reality he would face if he quit and went home now.

He replied as he wiped up his tears, "No, man, I should probably leave because that's the right thing to do. It's not about me and Ranger School. It's about my daughter, man."

I came back with, "OK, I understand, but what are you going to do for her now that you can't do a month from now when we're out of here? That's right, dude; we are halfway done with this shit. You know the truth. You won't admit it, though, so I'll say it for you. If you leave now, you'll never come back, and you know it. You know how bad it really does suck here, and you wouldn't come back. I wouldn't blame you, because I don't think honestly that I would come back either."

Germany finished wiping his tears and the snot off his face and said to me, "You're right, brother—you're absolutely right. OK, I'm good now. Let's get back to the platoon. We gotta prep for the field tomorrow. Thanks, man."

I said, "No problem, brother. I'm here for ya. Now let's get this field problem over with and get the fuck on to Florida and get this shit over with, right? Too easy, huh?"

He looked at me with a shit-eating grin on his face. "Way too fuckin' easy." We walked out of the woods together and never brought the subject up again.

CHAPTER 5

MOUNTAIN PHASE COMBAT OPERATIONS: TEN TOUGHEST DAYS IN THE ARMY

"Incoming!" the entire platoon shouted out and got down to the ground. The PL shouted back a distance and direction in response. "Twelve o'clock! 100 meters!" We were all running uphill, panting and gasping for air in full combat equipment, with the heaviest rucks one could imagine. The next whistling sound echoed through the misty wooded area. "Incoming!"

After the explosion went off, the PL sounded off again with, "Twelve o'clock! 100 meters!" This went on and was repeated for approximately a half hour straight, ever since we unloaded from the trucks at our debarkation point from the valley below us. It was uphill movement at a double time as we reacted to indirect fire. I guess we didn't move fast enough and with enough purpose for the RIs, as we un-assed the vehicles. Their most effective way for getting our platoon to move was to start throwing the artillery simulators.

When the indirect fire ceased, the platoon moved into a security halt. Accountability of personnel and equipment was priority first and foremost. The RIs designated at least two casualties along the way. One was walking wounded with minimal wounds, the other critical with a sucking chest wound. The medical evacuation (MEDEVAC) procedures started right away. This is how our field exercise began as soon as our feet touched ground out there after leaving Camp Merrill. I was glad I wasn't part of this initial leadership team being evaluated because it was pretty chaotic—just like combat, confusing and chaotic.

There was no "simulation" on the MEDEVAC, either. The platoon sergeant (PSG) and the medic found a nearby open area on the map, and two of us moved our wounded guy towards it with a security team attached. The medic and radiotelephone operator (RTO), overseen by the PSG, called in a standard nine-line MEDEVAC. No shit, within about ten minutes, a Blackhawk helicopter landed and we carried him to it and loaded him on. This was an actual MEDEVAC taking place right here in this school—no simulation with it whatsoever. I was impressed, and we were all made aware very quickly that we were not going to bullshit our way through this training exercise. Our radios, along with procedures, were being truthfully utilized up here, and were not to be taken for granted. There was not going to be any "checking the block," at least not for this field-training initiation portion.

The RI that was out with us for the MEDEVAC procedures did tell the student to get off the bird and go back with our group to the platoon area. His wound was "cured" and he was told to "Charlie Mike" (continue mission) with the rest of us. The procedures went off without a hitch, and I told myself that the PSG being evaluated would definitely receive a Go for this mission. Anyway, this was how our first hour kicked off for our ten-day field problem, and the instructors had all of our attention right off the bat.

Our first actual mission that we were to be conducting before the "indirect fire interruption" was a movement to contact, and to establish a patrol base, if memory serves me correctly. One thing is for sure: we moved all day and all night. By the time we did our leadership changeover, the platoon was already spent from moving up and down hills for hours upon hours. From here on out, the graded leadership positions were platoon leader, platoon sergeant, and the four squad leader positions. Everything else was assigned by the student leadership, or volunteered, but not graded, such as the team leader positions, RTO, platoon medic, and forward observer (FO). The bottom line was that everybody needed to do their jobs, volunteer, and give it all they got in order to take care of those that were being graded. Failure for just one student to do their assigned task, no matter what it may be, could result in mission failure. In this case, it probably would result in a failed grade for the other leadership positions. Everybody watched each other and got to know who was who, who was lazy, and who tried to give it their all most or all of the time. I say most of the time because everybody gets exhausted, and reaches their limit at times. To say not everybody falls asleep before, during, or after a mission is simply not true. Everybody will fall asleep in Ranger School—everybody is a human being.

We conducted patrol-base activities all night and well into the next morning as the sun was coming up. The first day of the field problem was behind us, but we felt like we had already been out there for days, if not a week. We got hit by small arms fire once or twice on the movement, conducted hasty attacks, and moved on. Once we established our platoon patrol base, the enemy hit us at least once there as well. It was pretty much nonstop, as expected. The Ranger School enemy or opposing force (OPFOR) were infantryman assigned to that particular training battalion. I suppose it would be a pretty decent assignment for a junior enlisted. They remained under the complete guidance and control of the RIs, and timely coordination with them was essential for our missions getting underway.

"What the fuck, Rangers? Why the fuck isn't anybody moving? You're only getting hit by the enemy, and nobody is doing shit! What the fuck?"

The enemy hit us very early in the morning, before sunlight, but who was counting days and keeping timelines by now, anyway?

"Rangers, I swear to God, if somebody doesn't start taking charge of this gaggle fuck, I'm gonna start throwing 'Arty Sims' on this perimeter!" Arty Sims, or "artillery simulators," were used on us if we were "not motivated" enough or simply not moving fast enough for the RI's standard. At the end of the day, they were absolutely correct, in that we were showing lack of motivation. After all, we were smoked and pretty much out of it for that initial forty-eight hours of the Mountain field exercise. When the instructors threatened to hurt grades if the platoon did not react appropriately to combat situations, you knew they meant business.

"PL, if you don't start making a decision and this platoon does not react to the enemy, every leadership position will fail this mission."

I remember thinking, *What mission?* We were technically on the same leadership positions from the day prior; there was no official changeover of leadership yet.

As soon as the threats came down from the instructors, leadership started making quick and fast decisions, and we maneuvered on the enemy with every weapons capability we had. We pretty much lit up the tree line, and the PL flanked a squad to maneuver and destroy the two OPFOR that were harassing us. Again, it went right by the book, with EPW and search techniques, proper reporting, and standard consolidation and reorganization after the assault.

"Hey, Rangers, keep fucking around and thinking this is some kind of game out here, and you all are going to be very disappointed with the end result, Rangers! Do not fuck around and hesitate again, Rangers, because you're fucking too tired and think somebody else is going to do your job for you again!"

We had received another eye-opener on just how serious these guys were on this training. By the way, we were a "nation at war" by this time, on two different fronts in the Middle East, too. So no shit the instructors were being serious about this, and I thought about how I was headed to Iraq to link up with my unit right after I got out of this school.

Once back at the patrol base and accountability was conducted, it was time for water resupply, and this shit was for real. Each squad was tasked to have at least one guy with an empty duffle bag to move out with the other squads' detail personnel to collect up each squad's canteens and move out with a security team to move down whatever high ground we were on and go to the nearest creek and fill up the canteens with fresh water. In the hills of northern Georgia, low ground always had some sort of natural water source. After filling up each squad's canteens, we would enter back into our patrol base and put one drop of bleach in the one-quarts, and two drops in the two-quarts. Each student had their canteens marked with their roster numbers so that we could easily identify our own. Too easy. Yeah, there were no water buffalos in the field in Ranger School during combat operations evaluations, at least not in the mountains of the Appalachian Trail during Mountain Phase.

After a routine morning check by the school medics on each of us in the platoon, it was on. "Roster Number Five-Zero—platoon sergeant!" I'll be damned; I received a planning-phase platoon sergeant position relatively quick in the Mountain Phase. I was actually feeling pretty lucky because for the most part, I was still very coherent and not exactly in zombie mode yet. Not to mention, planning-phase graded positions were an advantage too; you, as a student, had daylight. Usually when they called a changeover on you, during actions-on phase, it was during hours of darkness. In the Infantry, during combat operations, very seldom will any assault mission be planned to be executed during the hours of daylight.

So, I felt lucky. However, my game face was definitely on and no bullshitting. I got very serious, of course; who didn't when your roster number was called at any time for a graded position in this environment? Germany wished me good luck as I walked over to receive our operations order from the RIs, who had just changed out their shifts too. I believe their shifts in the field were twenty-four hours on, forty-eight hours off. That could have varied as well.

Depending on the mission or personnel count, it could have been twelve or twenty-four off. All I remember is it was twenty-four seven for us. I looked at my Ranger buddy and said, "I got this shit, dude."

"Let's go, Rangers. Get up here and get your briefing. We're burning daylight. We got everybody here?" They would always verify our roster numbers with our positions and make sure we understood completely before we received our mission briefing. It was an ambush mission on an enemy vehicle patrol, with approximately a four-kilometer movement. So we knew that meant we were going to get "hit" along the way, either by indirect fire, or personnel, or both. After the RI issued us our WARNO, we immediately began planning the mission, the movement, and of course, the timeline.

Once complete, along with the medic and forward observer I began constructing the terrain model while the platoon leader and squad leaders wrote the OPORD. Like I said earlier, by now we pretty much had this shit down to a science. However, never underestimate Murphy's Law when it comes to any military operation. Contingencies, contingencies, and more contingency planning is critical. This also included me as the platoon sergeant being prepared to take over as the platoon leader at any time from here on out, until our mission was over or until my evaluation time was complete.

After issuing the OPORD, going over the terrain model, and rehearsals on the mission itself, it was time to move out. I'll admit, I was nervous, because you never know what you're going to run into in this school. Taking this thing one step at a time was my goal, and getting it right was crucial if I was ever going to make it out of this phase.

It was around 0900 in the morning and relatively cold out. You could see your breath. Mornings like these, you just wanted to get moving in order to warm up a bit. Boy, did we end up "warming up" by the time this shit was over.

I moved up to the release point with the medic, and took a knee. It was fucking silent as all get-out. All you could hear was the sound of radio squelch and the chirping of crickets. I looked at my fingers and got disgusted by my cracked fingertips, caused by lack of vitamins and nutrition. We all saw our bodies deteriorating from lack of food and nutrition. I didn't think about my fingertips too long because the platoon was getting ready to move up in a file so the medic and I could count them out of the perimeter, one at a time. When Germany walked past us, I swatted him on the ass as I counted him. He turned and gave me the finger. Once everybody was out, I confirmed the count with the medic. Then my RI evaluator walked up and asked what I counted, and I confidently gave him my number.

"Are you sure?" he asked.

"Yes, Sergeant," I replied—confidently again. They always tried to make you second-guess yourself, but I had it right. He actually was cool and admitted I was right, that he just wanted to make sure I was alert. He shot the shit with me a little bit on the movement. Those guys, I'm sure, got bored a lot doing these missions time after time, cycle after cycle, and year after year.

About a click into the movement we got hit with small arms fire from the front of our formation. A click is military slang for a kilometer. We went right into react to contact/battle drill 2. The PL moved up to the front and assessed the situation. The weapons squad leader moved up and took control of the lead machine gun. The lead squad became the support by fire, and I quickly moved up with the rear gun and oversaw the support element while the PL moved back and grabbed the second squad in the movement, which became the assault element. He swiftly took them around and flanked. Once he got the assault squad in position, we shifted fire towards the opposite direction they were assaulting from. Once they got close enough to the three or four enemy personnel, I ordered the support by fire to lift fire, and then called the confirmation of the lift to the platoon leader so that he could proceed with the assault through the objective. Pretty textbook stuff.

Once they were through the assault and killed the enemy, we consolidated and reorganized around the objective. The PL called in the ACE (ammunition, casualties, and equipment) report with the number of enemy KIA. Luckily, the RIs assessed no casualties from our platoon. I'd say it went without a hitch. We recovered our rucks, I counted everybody out, and we moved out to continue mission. My evaluator walked up to me once we started walking again and gave me a little encouragement.

"Hey, good job back there, Ranger. You're looking good; keep it up." Without telling me, because they're supposed to wait until the end of the phase, he pretty much told me I was a Go. We hadn't had changeover yet, and I wasn't going to get ahead of myself, but man, I was feeling motivated and excited that I might be receiving a Go for my combat patrol in the Mountain Phase.

After about three hours of movement through the massive hills, we finally got close to our grid for the objective rally point, and went into a security halt. We then heard the magic words from one of the RIs, "Change of mission, Rangers." They called out the roster numbers for the leadership changeovers. Germany got picked to be one of the squad leaders for the actions-on portion of our ambush patrol. After we turned over equipment to the changeovers, I went back to a squad to be a rifleman for the remainder of the mission. My evaluator came up to me once everything got calm and took a knee next to me while I was in the prone pulling security.

"Hey, Ranger, you looked good, and I have no issues with your performance today. Keep it up, Ranger." That was it. Without my receiving an official pass or fail grade, he pretty much hinted that I would be receiving a Go on my patrol.

"Roger that, Sergeant," I said with enthusiasm. I was "done" with my grades in Mountain Phase. If I could have, I would have gotten up and started doing backflips around our security halt! All I had to do now, for the rest of this exercise, was keep motivated, help the platoon with anything they needed to help get the next guys through, and I would make it out of this phase successfully. I could even work off one if not both of the spot reports I had gotten from DSS in the mountaineering portion earlier. Damn! That seemed like a year ago by this time. For the next couple of missions, I volunteered to be team leader, carry one of the machine guns, you name it. I was so stoked!

The remainder of the mission was successful as well. I believe all graded positions received a Go, to include my buddy Germany. After it was over and we received our AAR, Germany came up to me, took a knee, and said the magic words. "Too easy, brother."

I replied, "Way too easy, Ranger buddy. I'm starting to believe that we're going to make it out of here."

We had a mission the next day where I volunteered to carry one of the M240B machine guns—heavy son of bitch. It was one of those movements where we had to climb a huge, steep-ass hill. This thing was so steep that it could have been considered a cliff. When we approached the base, we noticed there were ropes already secured to the top of it, so obviously it was a requirement for each platoon to climb up this thing.

"Oh boy," I said to myself as I looked up at this steep son of a bitch. I had the gun slung around the front of me, of course, with my eighty-pound rucksack on my back, and my LCE weighed at least twenty-five or thirty pounds with all my ammunition and water. *So, here I go*. I grabbed the rope and started pulling myself up, concentrating on putting one foot in front of the other. It probably took us about a half an hour to get to the top, but it seemed like two fucking hours. When we got to the top, the battalion commander and command sergeant major were waiting to greet us. "Good job. Keep it up, Rangers," the commander said to us.

A couple more days and missions later, we were in the patrol base. The sun was just coming up, and it was freezing. This phase had become an uphill struggle for me, and my worries were back on again. I'll explain because it could happen to any student this far in.

It was my turn to get off the perimeter, get to the center of the patrol base, and begin weapon maintenance on my M-4. I took my weapon apart and started cleaning it. While I was at it, I took a main meal out of my ruck and ate it in like thirty seconds. I ate it like I was going to prison. I was so hungry and tired.

After I put my weapon back together, I locked and loaded and went back to the perimeter to pull security. The medics were conducting their checks on the students prior to us receiving our next mission. The RI that graded me on my patrol a couple of days prior approached me, and, of course, I had fallen asleep.

"Hey, Ranger, how you doing?"

"Oh shit, I'm good, Sergeant, just fighting this sleep monster that keeps crawling on my back."

"Alright, Ranger, keep your ass awake. I know it sucks."

"Roger, Sergeant," I replied.

He then said, "Ranger, pull your charging handle back so I can check your chamber."

They did this to ensure that we remained locked and loaded at all times during combat operations.

I pulled it back and said, "See? I'm good, Sergeant. Always ready."

"OK, you're good, Ranger." As he started walking away, he came back and approached me again. This is when my world seemed to come crashing down, and the stress level went back up. "Ranger, look at your safety selection lever, and tell me what's wrong with this picture."

I had left my weapon on fire after cleaning it and didn't do my functions check like I've been taught and been teaching as an NCO for fucking years.

"Oh shit, Sergeant, I just literally got done cleaning my weapon and because I'm so smoked, I didn't do a proper functions check and left it on fire, Sergeant. I know I fucked up." I tried to talk my way out of this nightmare that I created for myself. The RI was writing me a major-minus spot report. "Oh no, please no, Sergeant; this will be my third one this phase."

"Ranger, sign here that you are receiving a major-minus spot report for having your weapon off safe within the patrol base."

I signed it as I continued to plead with him, but it wasn't working.

"Ranger, I don't want to hear any more of your shit. Think what would happen if you had a negligent discharge. You know the alternative from there, right?"

"Yes, Sergeant." The alternative would be an automatic day-zero recycle or go home. Day-zero recycle means just that. PT test and the whole nine yards. I don't think I would have been able to handle it at that point. I would have problems even passing the PT test with the state my body was in. So, three-quarters complete with Ranger School Mountain Phase, I received my third major-minus spot report, and my entire world collapsed in on me. I knew what I needed to do. Now I had no choice but to work off at least one of these before the end of the field exercise, or I would be facing an automatic board for phase recycle. What a dumbass I was and how I could make such a boneheaded mistake kept running through my head.

When the platoon received our mission and new leadership was assigned, I knew what I had to do. I volunteered to be the forward observer (FO) and carry one of the radios. It was a chance to hopefully receive a positive spot report, which would cancel out one of my negatives. As a matter of fact, I'd probably have to have a radio on my back as an FO or RTO the remainder of Mountain Phase. I was pretty confident that I could do it and pull it off. After all, we still had about three days remaining in the field.

As we moved out of the perimeter, I stayed close to the platoon leader, along with the RTO. About a kilometer into the movement, we got hit with indirect fire. After the PL got us out of the area and onto higher ground, the RI informed him that the indirect was coming in from a hilltop to our east, so we started plotting it on our map. I called in a fire mission according to the standard format that we carried on us. The RI was taking a knee next to me and the PL, observing me the whole time.

"Alright, PL, the enemy on hilltop such-and-such is neutralized—continue mission."

The PL replied, "Roger, Sergeant." Once we started moving again, I thought, *Man, I hope that was it. All I needed for a major plus.* Unfortunately, it never came. I would just keep driving on until it happened. I had to remain positive and focused on our missions.

After another mission of being FO, I honestly quit worrying about it and simply focused on completing this phase, which was a near reality for us, and hoping that the board members would waiver me from being recycled in Mountains. It is what it is, right? You could not "wish" anything positive from these instructors. It was either going to happen or it wasn't.

I volunteered to be a team leader for one of the guys that got picked to be a squad leader. He was nervous and a younger soldier. I was going to do anything to help him out and help him receive a Go. It was an ambush patrol, and we were to be set in by midnight I think. We were all in zombie mode with only one more twenty-four-hour mission after this one. When we got to the objective area and after we were set up waiting for the enemy vehicle, I moved up and down the line, making sure that everyone was as awake and alert as humanly possible.

When the vehicle approached, we engaged. The momentum was definitely not there; aggressiveness from the platoon as a whole was almost nonexistent. The RIs were pissed off and yelling out, "PL, this platoon better start getting aggressive on this fucking target!"

The firing of our weapons just didn't seem to be there. It was like *pop, pop, pop.* The M240Bs seemed to be jammed. The enemy dismounted and moved in on us, and the RIs did not assess any of them casualties, due to the non-aggressiveness our platoon was showing. Finally, one of the guns kicked in and started firing, and then one of the SAWs started firing as well. At this point they began assessing the enemy as killed. The PL ordered the assault element to move through the objective and get across the firebreak. As I came across, one of the bad guys jumped out from behind the vehicle, so I hollered out, "Close kill, close kill!" We were not allowed to fire blanks too close to them, especially at point-blank range, due to safety issues. We made it across the ambush area, and the PL designated our limit of advance (LOA). "LOA, LOA!"

Afterwards we conducted EPW and search and aid and litter on our casualties, and there were a couple of them. The less motivated the students were on missions, the more casualties the RIs assessed. And they were pretty pissed off after this particular mission. Once our left and right-side security linked back up with the rest of us, we went into our AAR, which turned into a complete ass-chewing. As I remember it, they even put us in the front leaning rest position while they were yelling at us.

"PL, that was weak as hell, and completely unacceptable! Rangers, you've been out here nine days now. You're hungry, tired, and your minds are all jacked up—I got it! We've been through it too, Rangers, or we wouldn't be here ourselves! You guys have a little over twenty-four hours left out here, so suck it up and drive on, Rangers! Alright, on your feet, men. PL, get us back to your fucking objective rally point."

Wow, I didn't know if he was a Go or No. I thought I was nervous for having three spot reports under my belt, but this guy was possibly looking at a patrol failure. If he went down, I wondered what that meant for the platoon sergeant and the squad leaders.

For the final assault mission the next day, I volunteered again to carry a radio, this time to change it up a bit and be the platoon RTO. It was a mission that I won't ever forget, because it included an experience I will never forget. I believe I ended up getting targeted by the RIs. I'll explain.

The mission scenario was that the enemy kidnapped one of our platoon members and was holding him captive. We were to plan and execute a raid on the complex in order to rescue him. It was the culminating mission of Mountain Phase. I remember it being pretty realistic as well. You could hear the enemy over loudspeakers give a speech over and over on how we Americans just "need to let it go" and get out of their territory. That bullshit echoed through the hills as we got closer to the objective. It actually was pretty eerie to listen to. Our minds were already playing tricks on us.

We moved into our ORP right at dusk and conducted our final mission preparations—re-camouflaging, taking off our patrol caps, putting on our helmets, putting on night vision, etc. The sounds of the speaker system grew louder and louder. I remember this so vividly. Our ORP was on top of a huge hill (of course they were all "huge" hills), and the objective was at the bottom. It felt like we were a mile up from it. I remember busting my ass on the way down at least twice because of the weight of our rucks, especially carrying a radio on top of it, with the extra batteries too.

The raid was successful and we got our Ranger back. Prior to our platoon AAR, we obviously had to go back up the hill to recover our rucksacks. Well, of course, me and the FO already had ours on. So I walked up to one of the RIs, who was a captain, and probably the company commander. I respectfully asked him if me and the FO could wait for the platoon at the AAR site since we already had our equipment on us.

He said, real sarcastically, "No, Ranger, you move your asses back up there with your platoon. You move with your platoon at all times."

"Yes, sir," I replied.

So, as we started heading up the hill, the FO said to me in a real low tone, "Hey, man, fuck this. Let's just hide out down here and wait for them to come back down the hill. Nobody's even going to know we're here."

I said, "No, man, we better do what we're told. I'm not fucking around with this place."

"Yeah, you're right about that. We've come too far to get into trouble."

So up the hill we went with the platoon. When we got up there, the captain was sitting down in our ORP, waiting on us. When I walked past him, he grabbed my leg and said, "Sit down next to me,

Ranger. I want to talk to you."

I said, "Yes, sir, what's up?"

"So, you thought you were going to try to trick us and stay down there, huh?"

"No, sir. It was mentioned, but we quickly decided to do what you told us and here we are—on top of the hill with the rest of the platoon like you ordered."

"OK, Ranger, I can't argue that, but you better watch your ass. I got my eyes on you. What's your roster number?"

"Five-zero, sir."

"OK, get out of here and head back down with the platoon."

"Roger that, sir."

At that point, I really wasn't concerned about it. I mean, after all, we did what the fuck he told us to do. Furthermore, I wasn't even the guy that suggested it, but I wasn't going to dime out the FO. That was the fucking problem with this place: others would in a heartbeat. It was a dog-eat-dog world in Ranger School. There were a few in each platoon that would dime out others to save their own asses. Either way, it wasn't me, but the problem with this whole thing was that this captain thought it was. I found out in the next three hours that it wasn't forgotten or going away after all.

After about two hours of sleep, the new RIs that were changing over came out to us. You could always tell they were in the area because you could smell them, as they were fresh and clean. I mean, you could literally smell soap and even deodorant.

"Where's Roster Number Five-Zero?"

"Here, Sergeant."

"Get up here, Ranger."

"Moving, Sergeant," I replied. It was a staff sergeant that I pretty much thought was a great guy up until this point. I approached him. "Yes, Sergeant."

"You know what, Ranger? You almost got your ass SOR'd this morning. You know that?" Then he repeated himself with a sarcastic look in his eye that I will never forget. "Yeah, did you hear what I said? You almost got yourself fucking SOR'd, Ranger. I think you'd better watch your ass from here on out."

I simply replied back to him with, "Yes, Sergeant." I didn't say anything else to him or mention doing what we were told or anything. I'm not stupid. I know what the fuck he was trying to get me to do. He was fishing for me to smart off back to him so that he could get me on a serious observation report, which, again, would mean automatic board to get released from school for an integrity violation. Nope. I wasn't falling for his bullshit. I simply kept my mouth shut and moved back with the platoon. I thought, *If I ever see that piece of shit back out in the Army, I'm going to fuck him up.* He was a dumpy-looking bastard. Back in the Army he probably wouldn't and didn't add up to shit. Oh yeah, some Ranger instructors were shitbags too. Not too many, but there were a couple hiding out in RTB for their NCO careers—like DSS back at Merrill.

Our final mission was a movement back to Camp Merrill and out of this godforsaken field exercise. It was basically just a planning phase with a movement. I'm sure it was also to provide a last chance for some of the students who still needed a Go in Mountains to get a passing grade. The senior RI on site was a sergeant first class, and he began calling out roster numbers and duty positions. "Roster Number Five-Zero—platoon sergeant!"

I said to myself, *What the fuck? I know I already got a passing grade because the RI who evaluated me damn near told me I did.*

OK, now I was worried again because I knew there were guys in this platoon that still needed a passing grade in order to get out of here. What I thought was transpiring looked more and more to be the case. They were targeting me. They were going to put me on this patrol as a graded platoon sergeant position, where I would receive a No-Go at the end, mark my word. I knew the system all too well, but I kept it to myself, and kept my mouth shut. We were probably going to get hit one last time—too easy. You really couldn't fuck this up, but they were the ones with the gradebooks. So, let's just see how this "movie" ends, shall we?

Without getting into the details of our movement, which was pretty basic and routine, we did get hit by small arms fire from a couple of OPFOR (opposing forces). We fought through them, defeated them, and there were no casualties on our end. After consolidation and reorganization, the medic and I counted the platoon out, the count was perfect, and we continued movement. After about a kilometer or so, the RIs told us "change of mission," and we would be moving the rest of the way back on a road in road-march formation. At that point I knew we were done with the field and we would be back in society soon. Thank God! However—and most people wouldn't believe this, but it happened—some poor bastard in the platoon had a negligent discharge with his weapon just before we entered back into camp. I shit you not!

Pow! His M-4 went off, and the RIs immediately stopped the formation.

"Alright, Rangers, who the fuck was it? Raise your hand." It came from the front of the formation, but they couldn't exactly pinpoint what student it was. He raised his hand reluctantly, but did so in good faith and without sugarcoating it.

"Here, Sergeant," he said.

"Alright, Ranger, you know what that means when we get back."

"Roger, Sergeant," he said disappointedly. I actually felt for him because he was a great kid and I believe he was smooth sailing up until this point. I looked down on my weapon and made sure the damn thing was on safe. Man, we were done too.

When we got back into Camp Merrill, I remember thinking how great it looked after the past ten days. I also remember wondering whether or not I was going to be recycled. At this point I was so hungry and tired, I just wanted something to eat and four hours of sleep. The RI that evaluated me on that final movement came up to me as we were still walking in and told me that he would give me my

AAR later after we turned in weapons and got cleaned up.

"Sounds good, Sergeant," I said to him. Actually, I wasn't worried about all that shit back there anymore. Hell, I was going to take a hot shower after ten days and get a hot meal.

After we thoroughly cleaned our weapons and equipment for two hours, we were finally authorized to turn them back in to the arms room. "OK, Rangers, get up to the barracks, wash your nasty asses and get into clean BDUs and boots."

Normally we would have run for the showers, but none of us had the energy to run. I wish there was a scale in those barracks. I would have loved to find out how much I weighed at that point. One thing about the latrine in the barrack at Camp Merrill that I didn't mention earlier: The stalls had mostly 187th Parachute Infantry Regiment (PIR) graffiti drawn all over them, pictures of Torres drawn with them. So, I pulled out my ink pin. I drew a picture of the 82nd Airborne Division insignia with my regiment below it. Too easy.

We formed up outside after we got cleaned up and were marched to the company headquarters where we conducted our peer evaluations, and yes, it was time for hot dogs again! This time we were authorized two hot dogs, a bag of chips, a candy bar and a soda to wash it down with. Again, I ate that shit like it was my last meal. Damn, they were the best hot dogs I ever ate in my entire life!

My state of bliss soon came to another crashing halt. Real calmly the RI approached me after I threw my paper plate away. "OK, Ranger, I have your AAR from the last movement done now."

"Roger, Sergeant," I replied.

"OK, Roster Number Five-Zero, your performance on the mission was substandard. You didn't do this and you failed to do that," was basically what he was telling me. "Overall you are a No-Go, Ranger." Yep, my instincts were right on! Those motherfuckers were targeting me. All because of that fucking captain after that final mission.

Again, I kept my mouth shut, and simply replied, "Roger, Sergeant." In the back of my mind I knew that I already had my Go on patrols, so that bullshit he just pulled on me was irrelevant. You only need ONE fucking passing grade on combat patrols in Ranger School. He was attempting to strike a negative reaction from me so that he could SOR me for disrespect or some shit. I had a Go on patrols, and I was pretty sure I was going to peer good again. The only thing I had to worry about were those fucking major-minus spot reports.

Afterwards it was time for us to receive our final phase counseling. Of course, guess who got to be the RI that counseled me? Yep, the captain himself. Joy! I took a seat in front of his desk, and I couldn't wait to hear what was about to come next.

"OK, Roster Number Five-Zero, you have a passing score on your graded patrol. You scored an 89 percent on peer evaluations. With that, you pass on evals. However, you have a total of three major-minus spot reports that you were unable to work off. Therefore, I will be recommending that you recycle Mountain Phase of Ranger School. Any questions?"

"No, sir."

"OK then, tomorrow morning after chow, you will report to the battalion commander, upon which he will determine whether or not you will be recycled or able to move on to the final phase. Again, any questions?"

"No, sir."

"OK, you're dismissed."

I stood up, saluted him and replied, "Rangers lead the way, sir." He didn't even reply with the proper response of "All the way." His return salute was half-ass too. This guy was a real piece of work, I'm not kidding. I said to myself as I walked back to the barracks, *Whatever, it is what it is. I'll find out my fate tomorrow morning, I guess.* I knew the reality of how this worked. If the BC decided that I would recycle, I knew I was never going to make it out of Mountains. When the next phase began, they would No-Go me on every test starting with mountaineering again. I got back to the barracks and went to bed. Was this going to be my last night in these barracks, or was I going to have to start all over again? I'd worry about it tomorrow. I was too fucking tired to give a shit now. I had a mattress to sleep on, for Christ's sake.

The next morning after chow, I walked over to the 5th RTB headquarters and stood outside the door. The captain came out and told me to go inside and report to the BC. He did not remain in; instead he went back to the company—thank God. I walked in, stood in front of the BC and rendered a sharp hand salute.

"Sir, Roster Number Five-Zero reporting as ordered, sir!"

He returned the salute and replied, "At ease, Ranger."

He had my file in front of him and was looking it over.

"OK, Ranger, your file says you passed patrols and received a high peer evaluation, but that you have three major-minus spot reports. Did you make an attempt to work those off in the field?" The command sergeant major (CSM) was standing off to the side. He looked really familiar too, like he had come from my brigade back at Bragg. Wow, that place seemed like a hundred years ago.

"Yes sir, I did. I volunteered all the time to be the RTO, FO, and team leader after I was complete with my patrol. I just never could receive a positive spot report for whatever reason, sir." I was getting very nervous, by the way.

"Ranger, what are your spot reports exactly for?"

"Sir, I received one for getting a No-Go on my initial belay test, one for a No-Go on my initial rock climb, and my final one was during the field exercise. I had my weapon on fire while in the patrol base, sir."

"It says here that you're an E-7, huh?"

"Yes, sir."

"I can see the first two spot reports, but that third one is ridiculous, especially for a senior NCO. What the hell was your weapon doing on fire in the patrol base for, anyway?"

"I had just got done cleaning my weapon, and didn't do a functions check after I put it back together, sir. I was just tired and smoked, sir, but no excuse."

He then went into my duty station.

"Where are you stationed at, Ranger?"

"Fort Bragg, sir."

"What unit?"

"3-505, sir."

He then looked at the sergeant major. "The 505th. Aren't they currently deployed, Ranger?"

"Yes, sir, they've been in Iraq for about two months now."

"OK, Ranger, so what you're telling me is, that there's a platoon over in combat right now without their platoon sergeant?"

"Yes sir. Immediately after graduation from here, I will be linking up with them over there." I started getting a vibe and a strong feeling that I was going to make it out of here.

He looked back over to the command sergeant major and asked, "What do you think, Sergeant Major?"

He replied, "Well, sir, under these circumstances, I think we can overlook and waive the spot reports." I started feeling motivated and confident again.

"OK, Roster Number Five-Zero, I'm going to let you move on to Florida Phase this afternoon. Remember, you being a senior NCO, the instructors are looking at you to be an example, so no more mistakes like leaving your weapon on fire. Had you had a discharge, I wouldn't be able to do anything for you—you know that, right?"

"Yes sir. I understand, sir."

"OK, Ranger, get out of here and go link back up with your company. I believe they're preparing for the jump into Florida as we speak. Also, good luck and go get down there in Florida, and get back to your platoon in Iraq."

"Thank you so much, sir." I turned towards the command sergeant major. "Thank you, Sergeant Major." I snapped to the position of attention, and rendered another sharp hand salute. "Rangers lead the way, sir!"

"All the way," he replied as he returned the salute. I did a right face, stepped off with my left foot and marched out of his office and the headquarters. Once outside, I threw my arms in the air, looked up in the sky and verbally thanked God.

CHAPTER 6

PARACHUTING INTO FLORIDA

After leaving the 5th RTB headquarters, I ran with excitement to link up with the company, which was conducting sustained airborne training, or pre-jump, down in the landing zone (LZ), just on the other side of camp. I sprinted down there with so much enthusiasm because the BC approved of me getting out of this forsaken environment of Camp Merrill and Dahlonega, Georgia. I first had to report back to the captain that had the issue with me and let him know that I would be leaving and jumping into Florida with the other sixty or so students that made it out of Mountain Phase. I couldn't wait to look him in his face and tell him the BC's decision, that I was moving on.

I approached him down on the LZ, saluted him and told him my good news.

"OK, Ranger, fall in the group. We're about to start pre-jump." Surprisingly, there was no attitude or sarcasm from him .

"Yes, sir," I replied, and then I moved out. I believed he was over it, and so was I. I got next to Germany.

"You get to come with us, brother?"

I replied with, "You know it! You know I ain't leaving my Ranger buddy." We all moved out and gathered in somewhat of a circle around the RI jumpmaster that was about to give us pre-jump. I looked around for the asshole staff sergeant that threw the term *SOR* in my face in the field, and I spotted him walking around. He saw me looking at him, too. He didn't say anything to me, nor did I to him. I simply wanted to get out of there and begin a new slate in the final phase.

After pre-jump, mock door training, and parachute-landing fall practices, we collected our duffle bags stacked up in the parking lot outside of the barracks. We loaded them onto a cargo truck that was headed down to Camp Rudder in Florida. We then rigged our rucks or ALICE packs to jump, and began painting our faces and necks. We loaded a bus and were taken to an airfield right outside the camp. We were so happy to be rolling out of there. The Bat Boys started singing their songs like the old days, and hell, me and Germany even joined in.

When we got to the airfield, we secured a main and reserve parachute. We didn't have actual weapons on us, obviously, so they had the M1950 carrying cases with two-by-fours in them to simulate the weapons, as they did in Benning during RAP Week. Damn! Did that seem like a year ago or what? It's all about the training, right? The RIs immediately had us don our parachutes, so me and Germany helped each other rig up. It was called "buddy-rigging." Afterwards, they began the jumpmaster personnel inspections, or JMPI. I was so motivated, I even asked if they needed help JMPIing the chalk, as I was a current and qualified jumpmaster myself. I knew the answer was going to be no, being a student myself, but I asked anyway. You can never have enough help; trust me, I know. If you read *Division: Life on Ardennes Street*, you'll understand where I was coming from. I don't think that my "buddy" the staff sergeant was jumpmaster qualified; he couldn't touch any of us during the inspections.

After the chalk was JMPI'd, we sat on the ground and waited for the aircraft to arrive, which was a C-130. If I remember correctly, only our chalk was jumping; there were only about sixty jump-qualified students getting out of this phase. The rest (maybe about twenty) that were not jump certified would be trucked or bused down with our duffle bags. I sat there thinking of the poor bastard that had that negligent discharge the day prior. He was probably getting ready to be bused back down to Benning to either be day-zero recycled or go home.

We loaded up the bird in reverse chalk order. Once seated, we were going to be in flight for about an hour, maybe an hour and a half (if memory serves me correctly). We sat down and it was nighty-night time for us.

We were awakened by the jump command, "Twenty minutes!" Then, "Ten minutes!" We then went into the ten-minute sequence before exiting the aircraft. The primary jumpmaster and his assistant on the other door gave all the jump commands, and us jumpers sounded off by echoing them. I remember thinking how relaxing it was to be "Joe Jumper" and not have the stresses of jumpmaster duty like I had so many times back at Bragg. Again, that world seemed 100 years ago.

Germany was in front of me. He turned around and said, "Have a good jump, Ranger buddy!"

"You too, brother!"

Then we both said it simultaneously: "Waaay too easy!!"

I heard the final jump command "Go!" As we moved towards the door, my heart started really racing, as it always does. I handed off my static line to the safety, turned in to the paratroop door, and exited. As I was blown through the air by the initial blast from the aircraft, I counted. "One thousand, two thousand, three thousand, four thousand!" My parachute opened and I was floating down over sunny Florida. As I floated towards the ground I thought, *Mountain Phase is* now *officially over.*

After my pretty soft landing, I removed myself from the parachute harness and "policed" up my equipment. I swear, it had to have been at least twenty or twenty-five degrees warmer than Georgia! Ahhh, man, if felt so good. I carried my parachute, reserve, ruck and my M1950 weapons case off the drop zone, turned it in to a crew that was at the leading edge, and was told to form up.

We were at Eglin Air Force Base in the northwest corner of the panhandle of Florida. We got on a bus that took us over to Camp Rudder, which was on the other side of the base and home of the 6th Ranger Training Battalion. I was nervous. Number one, about simply going to a new phase, but two, about whether I was going to have to put up with biased instructors like I had just encountered in the previous phase.

Hey, Nate, there's nothing you can do about it now. You're here now, and just take it one day, one task at a time, and you'll get out of here. And absolutely ZERO fucking minus spot reports. You have a "clean slate" down here. This is what I told myself on the bus ride into our new camp.

When the bus pulled into Camp Rudder, it stopped and let us off in front of our barracks, a three-story building painted in the "famous" Army light-tan color. Across the street were the two small company headquarters buildings. Down a little farther was the chow hall, which was next to 6th RTB headquarters, and across the street from that was the Gator Lounge, the little Camp Rudder bar and pub.

There was already a formation of recycles standing by, as there was for the first two phases. We got off the buses, and the senior RI, a sergeant first class, was standing there waiting on us.

"Go ahead and form up, Rangers. We're still waiting on your duffle bags to show up from up north. They should be arriving anytime now." After about a half an hour, I heard, "Roster Number Five-Zero, where you at?"

I sounded off with, "Here, Sergeant!" I ran up to the senior, stopped and went to parade rest. I worried what this was going to be all about. I hoped and prayed that all that drama from the Mountains wasn't going to follow me down here with these Florida Phase RIs. If it did, I'd definitely be screwed.

"We have to change your companies. You're now going to be in Bravo Company for this phase, OK?"

"Yes, Sergeant, but may I ask why?"

I was waiting for him to say, "No you may not, Ranger," but he didn't. Instead, he pulled me off to the side away from the formation and explained. "Hey, look, these are mostly recycles. We know what rank you are and what your duty position is back at Bragg. We're going to need your help with this group of students. They're mostly struggling. I'm actually putting you in a squad that has the most recycles from the platoon in it, so they're going to need your help in order for them to get out of here. So we expect your support and your help with them, Ranger, alright?"

"No problem, Sergeant. I'll do my best to help them."

He then asked me, "How's it going in that Panther Brigade back at Bragg, anyway?" I thought, *Wow, this guy really does know everything about me.*

I responded with, "Well, Sergeant, they're currently deployed to Iraq right now, and when I make it out of here, I'll be linking up with them over there." I made a point to emphasize the fact that I was linking up with them in Iraq as soon as I could graduate from this place—in case he didn't know, but he did. That was a good thing.

"Yeah, that's what I heard," he replied. "I was in 2 Panther before I got down here a couple of years ago."

"Oh, Airborne," I said.

I went back in front of the formation. I was relieved that, one, I wasn't going to be "targeted" by these RIs, and two, they counted on me to help out with my platoon and squad while we were going through this phase. What a fucking relief! At that point I felt so motivated again. After we got our bags and put our stuff up in the barracks, I ran into Germany, and explained to him why I left our company and platoon—that I wasn't in trouble or anything like that. He congratulated me, shook my hand, and we wished each other luck.

"I'll see you when we get done with this shit, man," he said to me.

"Yep, later, brother. Good luck to you." If I remember correctly, the other company, or simply two platoons, were on the floor below ours. When we all got back downstairs, we formed up and went over to the company headquarters building and began receiving our platoon equipment. Same procedure as before. Equipment draw, which included medic bag, VS-17 panels, a couple AT-4 anti-tank weapons, etc. Each of us also drew another sling rope and set of D-rings as well.

As it had the first two times, equipment draw and accountability of it all took about two hours. It wasn't that dramatic of an event this time, as it was in Darby and Mountains. I also noticed that for some reason the RIs seemed more hands off down here thus far. My new platoon seemed to be a bunch of good guys, and the same with my new squad. I remember feeling so at ease with everything down in Florida.

After we put our equipment up in the barracks, it was time for our first meal at Camp Rudder! We were starving (as usual). We hadn't eaten; at least, I hadn't eaten since breakfast up at Camp Merrill that morning before the jump. The chow hall was pretty awesome, and they fed us great too. Just like the other two phases, while we were training in camp we only ate two meals per day out of the chow halls. Usually breakfast and dinner.

For the next five days at Camp Rudder we performed some pretty long, drawn-out training, and had some really interesting classes. The first class was actually in the classroom. It was on the wildlife that we might encounter there in the swamp phase of Ranger School. This RI brought in this big-ass rattlesnake. It was the largest eastern diamondback I had ever seen in my entire life, and I had been to plenty of zoos across the country by this time. I couldn't believe how huge this thing was, and the RI just carried it around the classroom like it was a garter snake. Of course, there were some students that couldn't keep their eyes open during the class. The RI would tap them on the shoulder and tell them to wake up, and when they did, he'd have the rattlesnake's head next to them. It would scare the living shit out of them. One guy actually jumped up so startled that he fell on his ass. Of course, we all laughed our asses off. Good times.

They also brought in an alligator and some lizards. The alligator was just a baby, and another RI was handling it as well. Another snake they showed us that we definitely would and did encounter was the little pygmy rattler. When we got out to the field exercise, we found one or two under students' rucksacks throughout the ten days. That's why when you are out there, you always look under your ruck. At night you look under it with a red-lensed flashlight—always. I remember saying to myself, *I'll be damned if I'm going to leave Ranger School because of a fucking snake bite. The hell with my health; I want to finish this shit and get my tab.* They also warned us about the wild boar that were in the area, but hell, they were in every phase of Ranger School, not just Florida.

One class we pretty much used an entire day and half the night on was setting up and crossing a rope bridge—not a bridge that you could walk across, but simply a rope from one anchor point to another, in order to safely get a platoon across a river. During the upcoming combat-operations portion of the phase, there would be two missions that would have a river crossing where we would have to utilize this technique.

The class started with the RIs from our platoon demonstrating everything from beginning to end. First portion was learning how to properly configure and tie off our ropes around our chests and how to properly snap link into the main rope. We practiced until we all had it down, and then they came through and inspected each of us to ensure we did it correctly. After they demonstrated actually tying off the main rope and then simulated swimming across a large river and tying it off on the other end, they had us do it ourselves. Everyone in the platoon had to tie off until we all had it figured out. Same standard; the RI would verify each of us did it correctly without error. Each of us would then simulate swimming across and securing the rope on the other end. Then each in the platoon would snap into it and cross by holding on to and shimmying across the rope until we all got to the other side. Accountability of personnel (as always) was a must. Once on the other side, the platoon sergeant, along with the medic, would count each individual until the entire platoon safely crossed. For training on this task while on camp, we did this from one tree to another that was about thirty feet away.

It was imperative that each individual got this down to a science because it was known as a critical task. I believe in 1995 a few students had died during a swamp river-crossing mission due to hypothermia. So everybody took this shit very seriously. We practiced this, like I said, all day and most of the night. The RIs even had us doing it as a timed competition among platoons. We had it down pat. It brought more comradery to our platoon as well.

I got to know my platoon a lot better as the days went by, and they were good to work with. We asked each other what we did back in the Army, and what each other's rank was. It's kind of how everybody operated in Ranger School, at least in my class. Come to find out most if not all of my squad were second lieutenants in the Army National Guard. We all had something in common; they had just graduated from the Infantry Officer Basic Course (IOBC) prior to being here, as I did from ANCOC. Great bunch of guys—or so I thought, but I'll get into that later on.

Another good class was one on loading on and off and conducting boat operations. They trucked us out to a nearby lake and gave their demonstration and class. There was definitely an orchestrated, coordinated method of positioning on these zodiac watercraft. It wasn't simply "Everybody just get on and start paddling." Each craft carried a squad. There were set positions, to include the machine gunner up front on the bow of the boat. All our rucks were in the middle. Each Ranger, except the gunner, sat up with one leg inside the boat and the other outside in the water, as each paddled it through the water. It looked all intimidating and high speed, but it was an ass-smoker after you'd been paddling for six or seven hours. Again, during combat operations, there were three total boat movements, two of which had the river crossings integrated in them. Like I said, a total ass-smoker.

We spent like half a day on that, and it was back on camp doing tactical-rehearsals training. Pretty common in each phase. We rehearsed movement techniques, room-clearing techniques by fire team and squads, more rope-bridge rehearsals, you name it. This preparation for the field exercise went on for the first five or six days after our arrival to Camp Rudder. We'd eat about two meals a day, and get about three to four hours of sleep per night. Pretty standard for all three of the camps while we stayed on them prior to the field. You'd still lose weight due to the fact that you were constantly training and doing some kind of activity outside all the time. So you felt hungry all the time as well. By now, our bodies and minds were pretty much used to it.

Speaking of feeling hungry, for our last day in camp before heading out to the field, we didn't get breakfast in the chow hall. You would have thought someone killed my dog. I'm not kidding, we were depressed. Of course, we were already starving, tired, and had slight attitudes because we knew the dreaded ten-day field problem was coming up within twenty-four hours. I believe they were preparing us and putting us in starvation mode before we received our OPORD for our first mission. Honestly, I was looking forward to it, because it was our last field problem of Ranger School. Once we knocked that out, we were done and going back to Benning for graduation. We could do this—too easy.

Yeah right . . .

CHAPTER 7

FLORIDA PHASE COMBAT OPERATIONS: HELL WOULD HAVE BEEN A RESORT

The next morning, it was time to get our faces painted, get all our equipment and get outside. We would not see these barracks again for the next ten days. There definitely wasn't any mess hall chow today, either, but we already figured that. Instead, we marched out of Camp Rudder to our platoon planning bay area, and it began.

"Alright, Rangers, listen up for your roster numbers and duty positions. You all know how this works by now. Roster Number So-and-So, platoon leader. Roster Number Five-Zero—platoon sergeant!" He then called the four squad leader positions out. It was the same grading system as in the Mountains. The platoon leader, platoon sergeant, and four squad leaders. Everything else, such as team leader, medic, RTO, or FO, were extras and volunteer positions in order to help out and maybe try to receive a plus spot report. I was excited to get my graded patrol out of the way right off the bat, especially before I ended up in zombie mode like I knew I was going to be in the next couple of days. I figured that the RIs got mine out of the way first so I could concentrate on helping the others in the squad during the rest of the field exercise, as was mentioned to me when I first got to Florida by the senior RI. One thing was for sure, though; I was not going to fuck this up. I was going to do everything by the book and correctly. Remaining motivated would be my state of mind for this entire field problem.

We received our warning order from one of the RIs and went back to our platoon and immediately began the planning phase of our mission, which was a platoon raid on a small enemy complex. We also had a vehicle movement to our drop-off point. So I had to add a vehicle movement on our annex portion of our platoon operations order. The platoon sergeant is always responsible for writing this portion of the OPORD, and then overseeing the loading and unloading of each vehicle to ensure proper accountability. After we dismounted the trucks, we would have a five-kilometer movement on foot to our objective. Too easy. The terrain looked relatively dry for this mission—thank the Lord.

After I handed the PL my written portion of the OPORD, I went over with the medic and FO and began constructing the terrain model. Same standard as described earlier. We issued the order to the platoon and conducted rehearsals on movement techniques and actions on the objective. Once all this was complete, we loaded the LMTVs and moved out to conduct our first mission of Florida, or what was called the swamp phase.

We dismounted the vehicles, and the PL directed what direction we needed to move out. I checked all the vehicles to ensure no student remained on, perhaps fell asleep, and ensured nobody left any equipment. I gave a thumbs-up to the PL, went to the front of the platoon, took a knee, and the medic and I counted everybody out for our movement towards our objective.

About a kilometer into the movement, we got hit with enemy small arms fire to our front. Everybody immediately got down, took off our rucks and waited for the PL's directions. The lead squad got on line and began returning fire as per standard operating procedure. The PL moved up in order to assess the situation. He quickly made the decision to have the lead squad maneuver up and conduct a frontal assault by fire team. Apparently, it was two enemy personnel, and it seemed to be the fastest way to destroy them, instead of conducting a flanking movement. The two fire teams conducted three to five-second rushes while one team supported the other. Once one team was set, the other would move up. They did this until they assaulted through the bad guys and killed them. We then consolidated and reorganized, searched the dead bodies, sent up the report, and continued mission. The RIs did not assess any friendly casualties. It was pretty quick and to the standard.

After about another three and half kilometers, we went into our security halt, and moved into our objective rally point. I thought it went relatively smooth and without any issues or hiccups. It was still daylight, so we were moving a little bit ahead of schedule, and that was a good thing. The mentality in Ranger School was the faster you complete your mission, the more sleep you may be able to get.

"Alright, Rangers, listen up," one of the RIs sounded off. It was leadership changeover. After he gave out the new positions, he said, "OK, you guys go ahead and switch out your equipment and get yourselves squared away." It was pretty standard procedure, and we were all used to how this worked by this point. Nothing came as a surprise—yet.

The RIs took former leadership off to the side and gave us our after-action reviews individually. My instructor gave me pretty much all good remarks, but I was still nervous. I mean, it was natural in this environment to want to know if you passed or failed.

I asked, "So, Sergeant, what do you think—"

He quickly cut me off. "Hey, Ranger, did I tell you that you needed to improve on anything?"

"No, Sergeant."

"OK then, that should tell you all you want to know. Now, you help your squad out because they're going to need all the help they can get, you hear me?"

"Roger, Sergeant, and I will," I replied. Fuck yes! It happened again! Without telling me whether I officially passed, he pretty much hinted that I was a Go. I said to myself, *That's it! I did it! I just got a Go in Florida phase.* I was so stoked and pumped up. I promised myself that I was going to bust my ass to help my squad and the rest of the platoon out. I would volunteer to help wherever they needed me from now until this field exercise was over—and I did.

I went back to the platoon and asked if any of the squad leaders needed a team leader or anything else.

"No, we're good; thanks, man. You just got done with your graded patrol. Take a break and just be a rifleman in your squad. Maybe next mission, brother."

This is what the new platoon leader told me in front of the squad leaders.

"OK, just let me know how I can help."

They were good guys, and we were taking care of each other, but in the next couple of days, it got really rough. However, that was to be expected. After all, we were in the "run phase" of this program, and we knew it was going to be the hardest.

A couple of days and a couple of complete twenty-four-hour missions later, it was time to knock out our first mission that had a boat movement, major swamp movement by foot, and a river crossing to boot. We were so hungry and tired. It was going to be another platoon raid on a small enemy complex. Most of our missions during this phase were raids, with extremely long movements to each objective. Also, by this point in Ranger School, we all started noticing something else. There was a strong, odd odor in the air, but I had heard about this throughout the years prior to making it to this course myself. The odor was ammonia, and it got stronger the closer we got to one another. It was the smell of our muscle tissue burning in our bodies. After the body burns most of its fatty tissue, and there's no more to burn or very little left, it begins burning muscle.

The smell is literally the stench of ammonia. So be it; suck it up and drive on. We had to get through this next tough mission.

After the OPORD and rehearsals, we loaded trucks and headed towards the river. We got to the riverbank, secured one zodiac watercraft per squad, and began loading them. Each zodiac had an RI on board, sitting on a little fold-out stool in the back of the boat. RIs with their little folding chairs were a pretty common sight, and they usually carried them on the back of their LCEs each mission. Also, it was common down in Florida to see them moving with walking sticks too. The walking sticks were nicely carved out, usually with some kind of design on the top.

We began moving down the river, and as we did, everybody was quiet and remained tactical. I remember thinking, *Now, this is some real Ranger high-speed shit.* After about two hours of paddling, it started to suck. It was kind of funny, because as we moved in silence, you could hear stomachs growling. Then, as we went around this particular corner, one of the funniest, most memorable comments and moments happened during my time in Ranger School. There was an older guy in a small boat fishing. With him he had a small chihuahua sitting up and staring at us as we paddled by.

"You boys in the Navy?" he asked.

The Ranger behind me replied, "No, we're in the Army."

Then it happened. The guy in front of me looked at the man and asked with a real strong Southern accent, "Hey—what you gonna do with that dog?" Everybody on our boat quickly turned towards the older man and waited for his response. He never offered one. We went about our business and continued paddling on. About a minute later, when we were away from him, the RI busted out in laughter.

"Rangers, do you all realize what the fuck you just asked that old man?"

"Roger, Sergeant. We wanted to eat his fucking dog."

I swear we would have in a heartbeat. One thing you realize in this school is that human beings are animals too, and you will eat anything when you're literally starving.

After about six hours of moving down this fucking river, we arrived at our debarkation point and would move the rest of the way on foot to our objective. It was probably around 1300 or 1400, and we would not see dry land again until well after dark. We remained in waist and chest-deep swamp water this entire movement until we got to the river we had to cross. Everybody fell down periodically from tripping over tree roots that we could not see under the water. These swamp movements were definitely the worse of any phase. I'd rather have been moving through the mountains again. At least we could see what we were stepping on or through. The guy in front of me turned and told me, "Hey, dude, I just shit my pants, so move out of the way." I didn't care at this point because I just wanted this movement to be over with and couldn't wait to see dry land again. By now, nobody would have a solid shit anyway. I know I didn't.

After about four or five hours, we made it to the river. Since we'd been submerged in water, the only sign we were at the river was that it was a wide-open area. We wanted to get across it before it got dark, and we were cutting it really close, as it was dusk already. We didn't waste any time at all. The rope man swam across the river with a security guy. There was a boat standing by with instructors and medical personnel aboard for safety purposes. Remember what I mentioned earlier about the students that had died out here about seven years prior. The cadre took no chances with our safety, especially since it was late October and the temperature was a lot cooler.

Once the rope was secured and tied off to the anchor points, we tied our sling ropes and secured them around our chests, and made sure our wet-weather bags were tied up completely inside of our rucks, in order to ensure our gear inside would remain dry while we crossed. We all went one at a time, snapped into the rope, and began shimmying across the river. Man, it was deep, and those eighty-pound rucks would weigh you down. The goal was to get across as quickly as possible, get out of the river, and get counted out by the platoon sergeant. Once we all got across and were counted, we moved into a security halt on a nearby area of higher ground. Finally, we made it to dry land!

Once in the security halt, the RIs made us all change into dry uniforms in order to prevent hypothermia because the temperature was dropping, as it was already completely dark. They then called off the next chain of command for the actions-on portion of our raid mission. We were smoked, especially after six hours on the river and that bullshit five-hour movement through the swamp. We definitely were not looking forward to doing that again. At this point, I don't think any of us knew what day we were on or how many days we had left of this field problem. I'm pretty sure the previous leadership were all Gos on the planning and the two major movements because everything seemed to go pretty smooth, with the land navigation and the river crossing. I can't say the same for the actions-on leadership that night. Our first river-crossing swamp movement was a failed mission for the actual raid portion. I'll explain.

Once the equipment was turned over, the PL told the RIs we were prepared to move out. The platoon sergeant counted us out, and we began moving again. I think we had like a three or four-click movement. We didn't get too far, and we were already heading off course from our azimuth we were supposed to be on. The assigned platoon leader for this portion did not correct the direction we were moving, and the RI had to correct him. I'm not going to sugarcoat it; we were all walking zombies at this point.

"PL, what azimuth are you supposed to be on?"

"Such-and-such degrees, Sergeant."

"Well, are you fucking aware that you're not even close to that right now?" He halted the patrol and got with the point man and checked his compass, and thought he had him straight. I walked up to the PL and asked if he wanted me to take over as the Alpha team leader and take point. He came back like an ass and told me no, that he wanted to keep his buddy up there.

"OK, roger that," I told him. I think they were lieutenant buddies, and I was all right with that. It wasn't my patrol. I tried—right? Anyway, we started moving again, and within a matter of minutes, we were off azimuth again.

"That's it, PL, stop! Everybody just fucking stop! That's the third time we're off course, Rangers! PL, this is your last chance to get this platoon moving in the right fucking direction. I'm going to tell you that right now." I would have taken that as a hint that maybe it was time to find a new point man, but I knew what he was doing. It was his Ranger buddy, and he didn't want to offend him. In this place, you had to do what you had to do sometimes for the good of the mission, or it was going to cost you and the rest of the leadership. For this mission, it did just that.

We went off course again for the fourth time, and the RIs had enough. "Stop, Rangers! Just stop! This is a failed mission, PL. Your platoon has failed to move in the correct direction four times now, and you didn't do shit about it. Rangers, give me a patrol base right here. PL, once you're properly set in, put them to sleep."

I remember feeling bad, but I offered to help and was pretty much told to fuck off. Too easy. Once in my position on the perimeter, I pulled my poncho liner out of my ruck, and pulled out my wet boots and wet uniform from the previous movement to dry out. I used my field jacket liner as my pillow on my kidney pad on my ruck, threw my poncho liner or wooby on top of me, and it was nighty-night time. Yeah, I felt bad because I just watched all the leadership get a No-Go. I felt bad for about thirty seconds and fell asleep. It was about 0100 in the morning. Our hit time on the objective was supposed to be an hour ago, but we didn't move more than a click and a half before they finally stopped us. Welcome to the reality of Florida Phase.

About four hours later, the instructors woke us up. We could smell the fresh soap and deodorant, so it must have been their RI changeover. "Let's go, Rangers. Get around, conduct personal hygiene and re-camo your faces. The medics will be around to check on you all. The same leadership will remain in place." I remember thinking that it was cool that they were going to get another patrol—this time planning.

"PL, you're not getting your next mission until this afternoon. This morning the platoon has a survival class."

After the medics checked us, we packed up our gear, and the RIs led us out to a nearby firebreak. We walked down it for about an hour and got to our destination around 0900. "Ground your gear in formation, Rangers, and get into the bleachers."

It was an outdoor classroom setting—a set of bleachers with an overhead cover. Pretty standard to see throughout all three phases. It resembled a planning bay for field operations. Off to the side was a wild boar hanging on a wooden structure. It had been already gutted and cleaned, and looked like it was ready to cook and eat. We were so excited because we thought we were going to be able to eat it. That is what we all thought during this entire first class.

We received a full block of instruction on how to gut and clean the boar, but like any other class in Ranger School, it was hard to keep your eyes open. The thought of being able to eat this thing kept most of us awake and excited to be there, doing something other than walking through the woods or the swamps. When the block of instruction was over, the RI giving us the class gave us all some very disappointing news.

"You won't be able to eat any of this, Rangers! About ten years ago you could have, but now the Army says we have to feed you domesticated animals for this class."

The whole platoon at the same time cried out, "Awwww."

Another RI walked out in front of us with a chicken in his arms, and he was petting it. "This is the domesticated animal that you will be eating today, Rangers! It is a nice chicken. Plump and very lively, Rangers! One thing about this animal that makes it very easy to kill, Rangers, is that it's head will come off relatively easy!"

He then grabbed the chicken's head as he was petting it and ripped it clear off and threw it over our heads.

"Oh shit!" we all cried out, because it was a shocking moment that we weren't expecting. He then placed the chicken, as it was still kicking, upside down in a coffee can to allow the blood to drain out of it. It lay in the coffee can kicking back and forth for about fifteen seconds before it finally was dead. Now I learned where that "running around like a chicken with its head cut off" phrase came from. He then gave us the class on how to properly clean it.

Once that class was complete, the instructors gave each squad a live chicken, and it was time to go to work. Each squad received the chicken, about three coffee cans, a five-gallon container of water, and a bunch of carrots and sticks of celery. It was awesome; the RIs actually brought us carrots and celery to go with our chicken! This was heaven!

I grabbed the chicken, secured its legs with my hand, put my boot on its neck and pulled up, popping its head off like a dandelion. Then I placed it upside down in one of our coffee cans. Once it was dead, we wasted no time. We began cleaning it, ripped off its feathers and chopped it up. Other squad members chopped up the vegetables. We were going to make ourselves some homemade chicken soup, goddamn it! We set the three coffee cans over our little fire and boiled the pieces of chicken and the vegetables in the water. We made sure it was cooked thoroughly enough, and then everybody got our canteen cups and an MRE spoon out and went to town. Everybody in our twelve or thirteen-man squad got an even cupful. I took out some hot sauce and a salt packet and had myself a nice cup of hot, fresh, chicken soup. It was awesome, and us starving grown men didn't even fight over the chow like I thought we would. There was good comradery among our squad. We talked about what the RIs were going to do with that wild hog. We knew they were going to have a cook-out with it, and that it wouldn't go to waste. Man, we wished we could have been a part of that one. Anyway, we ate our canteen cups of chicken soup like we were going to prison or it was our last meal.

After the little "treat" of our survival class, it was back to combat missions and the bullshit. It was time for an operations order, planning, rehearsals and a long-ass movement with another raid mission. Like I said earlier, the instructors left in the same leadership that had the failed mission last night, which was pretty cool. They all got another chance, and we were going to pull together to help them be successful. Especially now that we had four hours of sleep and food in our stomachs! We were motivated to get going with the realization that we were closer to getting out of this field problem. I believe, if memory serves me, we did the mission with no issues, and the leadership were probably all Gos.

The next day's mission was our second boat swamp-movement river-crossing mission. This time they added a helicopter insertion along with it. We were dreading it after we received the order. We had it in our minds that this was going to be the ass-smoker of all ass-smokers. Come to find out, it wasn't as long or grueling a movement by boat or foot as the first water mission. The boat movement was about two hours, and the swamp movement was about another two hours. We knocked out the river crossing with no issues. This mission got started a lot earlier than the first one did, too. We were on the river in our zodiacs as the sun was coming up, and we were across the river by around 1700 hours. Once on dry land again, we changed into dry uniforms and headed for our landing zone to get picked up by the birds. Once at the LZ, the RIs did the leadership changeover, and we were to conduct another raid on an enemy complex after landing. At this point, I was so weak that I could no longer put my rucksack on over my head and slide my arms through the shoulder straps, like I had up until Florida Phase. Now, I had to sit on the ground and lean back and slide my arms through the straps, tighten them down and have another Ranger pull me to my feet.

Once the choppers landed, we boarded and buckled ourselves in. We were on UH-60 Blackhawks, and I will never forget what came next. I had heard rumors about this in the past, but had kind of forgotten up until this point because we were so smoked. The pilots brought each of us a bag of McDonald's. In each bag, we had quarter pounders, fries, and a Snickers candy bar. You would have thought we all died and went to heaven—I'm not shitting you. As a matter of fact, I remember almost seventeen years later that my Snickers candy bar was in the yellow wrapper, which meant it was a Snickers with almonds. That is how vividly I remember this meal.

The pilots told us we had to eat it all before we took off. Shit, they didn't have to worry about that! We ate that meal like someone was going to try to take it from us. This meal from the pilots was a Ranger School 6th RTB tradition that dated back to the sixties. I'll explain. This particular flight unit had a helicopter crash, and a platoon of Ranger students were in the area and came to their rescue. They ended saving and pulling the pilots from the crash site. So, it is a tradition that the pilots pay back each Ranger class with a meal in appreciation. That's a true story.

After a couple more days and a couple of missions, we were almost done with the field exercise. We were on our final mission of Florida Phase, and our final twenty-four hours out in that shit. This was the final, biggest mission of Ranger School. A long movement into a hasty defensive position. From there, we were to move out and conduct a vehicle movement, a boat movement across the Gulf of Mexico (about a mile or so), land on Santa Rosa Island, conduct a raid on the enemy headquarters compound, and, finally, conduct a helicopter extraction. At this point, being at our end and so tired and hungry, I was glad my leadership graded position was over—or was it? One of the most shocking and depressing moments of my experience in Ranger School was about to happen.

After we walked all day and arrived to our patrol base location, we were to dig hasty fighting positions and partner up with another student for security. Once we got ours dug and were set in, I pulled out an MRE and began chowing that son of a bitch down, like it was my last meal on death row in San Quentin Prison. It was dark by this time. I got done with my main meal, and started pulling security so that my Ranger buddy could eat his.

We were waiting to hear the changeover roster numbers for the actions-on leadership change. The RI began calling out the numbers for our final mission. "Roster Number Five-Zero—platoon sergeant!"

I looked at my partner and said, "Wow, it sounded like he said Roster Number Five-Zero."

He replied with a sad tone, "Ah, he did, brother."

"What the fuck?" I immediately started feeling sorry for myself and got sick to my stomach.

"Let's go, Rangers, get up here and get your changeover!" Since it was dark, he sounded off with our roster numbers to ensure we were all there. I mean, it was dark as shit. You couldn't see two feet in front of you.

"Roster Number Five-Zero."

"Here, Sergeant."

"Don't sound so sad, Ranger. It's your final mission." He then pulled me off to the side. He explained to me, though I pretty much already knew the deal, "Hey, listen, Five-Zero, the PL is going to need your help to get him through this. He already has a failure this class, and as I'm sure you already know, these guys are mostly recycles. So we need you to help get him through, Ranger."

"Yes, Sergeant," I assured him.

"Alright then, get your equipment changed over and get everybody prepared for move out."

"Yes, Sergeant."

"Damn it," I said to myself. Man, this was a vehicle and boat movement across the fucking ocean (at least a mile), the mission itself, and then a HELO extraction to boot. I had my work cut out. Arrive at the cutting edge of battle by air, land, and sea, right? "OK,

Nate, suck it up and quit feeling sorry for yourself, motherfucker," I told myself. "You have a job to do, so make it happen and you'll be out of here once and for all."

When the LMTVs pulled up, we got everybody loaded up, and I got accountability and let the PL know we were good to go. He gave the report up to the RI, and we moved out for our final mission of Army Ranger School.

After about a half-hour drive, we got to the beach. Each squad unloaded our zodiacs off of a parked trailer that was there waiting for us. I got accountability of the platoon, reported it, and we began loading the boats. I was very careful and paid close attention to detail. After all, it was dark (very dark), and I was at my end, both physically and mentally—we all were. I'm sure that's just the way Ranger School wanted us at this point.

We paddled to the island. This was actually a battalion mission with each company having their own mission and section of the compound to assault. Our platoon's portion was to clear and secure the first two buildings. The boat movement actually didn't take as long as I thought it would. A mile and a half or so doesn't take long to get across. The water was pretty calm, believe it or not. I was impressed by how smooth this operation was going thus far, but it wasn't going to be smooth for long.

We landed on the beach and began our assault on building one. We set up a support by fire on one of the larger sand dunes, and then, once set, the PL took up the first squad and went to enter the building. At this point, we weren't taking fire and seemed to have the element of surprise, so we did not open up with the guns as the initial squad moved up. Once they got close enough, the enemy began shooting at them. We opened up on the building to the left, while they moved around to the entrance of the target building on the right. Once inside, the next squad moved up to enter the building. I left with them because we started getting casualties within our platoon, and I needed to establish a casualty collection point (CCP). When the second squad entered the building, I asked what room was secured first. I marked it as the CCP with a red cross made with red chemical lights.

It happened so fast that by the time we were in the building, it was secured, but chaotic with screaming. There were already enemy prisoners being guarded, and while the medic was triaging the couple of casualties we had, I called up the third squad and told support by fire to collapse and enter the building. The next building needed to be assaulted; we were starting to bunch up inside building one.

The PL was fucking around with the prisoners and worried about our casualties that the medic was tending to.

I told him, "Hey, PL, you need to take the next squad and begin your assault on building two!" He wasn't moving. I commanded, "Second and third squads to line up and prepare to take building two! Weapons squad will secure outside and the couple rooms in here! Let's go, sir. You need to move out with the assault element on the next building. We're losing our momentum, goddamn it!"

The RI was standing there just watching and observing our situation.

I then commanded, "Second squad, begin your assault on building two! PL, you need to follow and command them!" He was still so worried about the casualties and prisoners. Totally in my Kool-Aid, and I was getting more pissed off by the second. I walked over to him, grabbed him by the back of his LCE, and picked him up and practically threw him out the fucking door after the assault element.

Second and third squads cleared the second building and took another two casualties. The medic and I went over and picked them up and brought them back to the CCP in building one. Each squad gave their reports over the radio. I walked back to the second building and grabbed the couple more enemy they captured and brought them back with a couple guys to watch them from third squad. We consolidated and reorganized, called in the MEDEVAC for our casualties, and the walking wounded were simply going to fly out with us. Our portion of the objective was secured.

The senior RI that overwatched our platoon sounded off with, "Change of mission, Rangers! PL and platoon sergeant, get accountability of all equipment and form them up out back."

"Roger, Sergeant, WILCO!" WILCO is radio lingo for "will comply." That was pretty much it for our last mission, other than the flight out back to Camp Rudder.

"OK, Rangers, somebody get your platoon out on the road behind this village, and move them down until you get to the clearing. Once there, stand by for us to link up with you all."

"Roger, Sergeant," we replied. He came back over to me and told me to stand by, that he wanted to talk with me on the way out there one-on-one. I remember thinking, *Now what?*

"Yes, Sergeant," I replied to him.

The platoon headed out to the open beach area down the road. Once they left, me and the senior instructor took off about ten minutes behind them. He just wanted to shoot the shit with me, because he too was assigned to my regiment back at Bragg prior to him coming to 6th RTB.

"Hey, good job back there, Ranger. You did a strong job."

"Ah shit, I thought I was in trouble for being a little rough on the platoon leader during the assault. How did he do, by the way?"

"He'll probably pass, thanks to you getting him out of that first building. I'm telling you, if he didn't go, he would have been a No-Go."

"Alright, that's good. I don't want to see him fail, especially since I was assigned to help him pass."

He was a good instructor, and was cool with me. After all, realistically he knew what rank I was. It wasn't favoritism, either. I believe I did a good job during this phase and helped out as much as I could. Anyway, we finally linked up with the rest of the platoon as the sun was coming over the ocean.

"OK, Rangers. Everybody go ahead and relax. You all did a pretty good job last night. Sit back against your rucks and enjoy the view. It's going to be a little bit before the birds arrive, Rangers."

I sat there on the white-sand beach, leaning up against my ruck. We all simply stared out at the ocean as the sun rose. The seagulls flew overhead, and waves crashed against the shore. It was one of the most peaceful scenes and moments of my life. I was in a state of euphoria as I stared out on this beautiful moment.

It's over. It's all over. No more worrying about getting through this school. No more dick-measuring contests back in my unit at Bragg. These were the thoughts running through my head. I also wondered how my Ranger buddy, Germany, did during this phase. I'm sure he did just fine.

Two CH-47 Chinook helicopters landed behind us on the other side of the small road.

"Alright, Rangers, everybody police up your equipment and load up the aircraft. We're headed back to Rudder!" We all cheered and clapped, got our shit on, got into two single-file lines, and boarded the aircraft.

Once back on Camp Rudder, we all marched over to our classroom, the same one where we had received the animal class prior to heading out to the field. We grounded all our equipment except for our weapons and went inside the classroom to conduct our squad peer evaluations. After every phase, that was the very first event they had us complete prior to anything else. The logic being they wanted all events to still be fresh in our minds.

"Alright, Rangers, you know the deal by now. Be honest with yourselves and with your squads when filling out your peer ratings, and stay awake. Wake up back there, Ranger!" We were smoked, and it was difficult to keep our eyes open. All we cared about was getting our end-of-phase hot dog meals.

After we were done with our peer ratings, we went outside, secured our equipment and were told to head back to the barracks to get cleaned up. We got showered up, and put on fresh BDUs out of our duffle bags. Those hot showers after coming out of these ten-day field problems were the best, as expected. We got back outside the barracks and formed up with our weapons. We were told to begin cleaning our squad and platoon equipment and not to worry about our weapons yet; that would be later. Man, we just kept thinking about our hot dog dinner.

That afternoon, the RIs started calling us into our company headquarters to receive our final-phase after-actions reviews while we were cleaning our equipment outside.

"Roster Number Five-Zero, come on in, Ranger." I went running across the road and into the building. I was feeling so good, nothing like I felt when I was about to receive my final review in the Mountains. I knew I had two Gos during my combat patrols, no spot reports, and I was sure I was going to get a high peer rating, especially after helping out as much as I did.

I was gravely mistaken.

"Have a seat, Ranger." It was the sergeant first class that graded me on the final patrol from the 82nd. "OK, you got two passing grades on patrols, zero negative spot reports." I noticed he didn't mention peer evaluations yet. "You got peered last, Ranger. You will be boarded by the company commander first thing tomorrow morning."

I looked at him with the biggest look of confusion. "What the fuck, Sergeant? What's this shit all about?"

"I guess they got pissed off at how you were up their asses on that final mission. Again, I'm guessing."

I sat there in such disbelief and disgust with those motherfuckers. I just put my head down, crossed my arms, and began shaking my head. All I could think about was going back outside and beating the fuck out of every single one of those buddy-fuckers.

He began to reassure me. "I'm going to talk to the senior instructor after this and then we're going to talk to the CO. We're going to explain what exactly happened, and that we both believe that they tried to fuck you in order to save their own asses on the peer evals. I wouldn't worry too much about it tonight, or lose any sleep over it. I think you're going to be alright, Ranger.

"Also, DO NOT go back to those guys and start any shit with them whatsoever, like I know you want to. I can see it in your eyes. Don't worry, Ranger, I'd be pissed too. You and So-and-So are the only enlisted in the squad, and they tried to peer you last. We were with your platoon the entire field problem, off and on, and you did a good job, like you were asked in the beginning of the phase. Now, I'm not going to sit here and guarantee you that you won't get recycled, but I think you'll be alright. Now, you go start any shit with them after this, you sure as shit will get into trouble and not only recycled, but probably even worse than that. So, keep your head cool and just ignore them. OK, Ranger?"

I looked at him still shaking my head and replied, "Roger, Sergeant." I then got up and walked out.

I didn't go back to my squad and platoon. Instead, I went straight to the barracks and paced around our bay in disbelief, talking to myself. How the hell could they have done this to me? I mean, the platoon leader got a Go because of my actions. How did I know for sure? The fucking RI told me to my face that he was going to be alright. And to think, I was actually worried for the little prick.

This was the reality of Ranger School. Not only do the students have to worry about meeting the standard on all the tasks, but the *real* worry is getting on the bad side of the instructors and/or your student peers. First, I had to worry about not getting out of Mountain Phase for pissing off those couple of asshole RIs at the end, and now I had to worry about getting out of Florida because of this handful of National Guard lieutenants. Why? Because I hurt their feelings on the final mission? I guess I yelled at them too much to do their fucking jobs, right?

"OK, Nate, shake it off, and get your ass outside. Don't say a fucking word to those fuckheads. Just finish cleaning the equipment and get the shit turned in, and then you can go enjoy your hot dogs."

When I got back outside and linked back up with the squad, nobody said shit to me, but I waited for it. I was going to keep my cool, just like the RI warned me to. As a matter of fact, none of those cowards would even look at me. The RIs continued to call more students inside to give them their AARs. I remained quiet and professional as I could be under the circumstances.

After we turned in our platoon equipment, I walked over to the other company and linked up with Germany. He got an overall Go in the phase, and Ranger School as a whole. I was happy for him, but I would have been happier if I knew what my future was going to be. All I knew was that if I had to recycle this phase, it was going to be the end of me. It was the worse ass-smoking I took the entire course, and definitely throughout my twenty years in the Army. I'm not lying, either.

At this point, I simply stayed with my Ranger buddy the remainder of the night, and stayed away from that platoon and fucked-up squad of mine. I told him the story about what I had to deal with, and he couldn't believe it. He then told me not to worry about, that the RIs were going to "have my back."

I said, "Yeah, you're right. Let's get our hot dog meal." We got three hot dogs, a bag of chips, and a candy bar this time! We ate them as if we were the shark and the hot dogs were the little boy on the raft from the movie *Jaws*.

They fed us outside the Gator Lounge, on the patio. The RIs even let us go inside and have a couple of beers. It was heaven on earth. I think I had three beers. Although I could have stayed in there all night, I figured I'd better cut myself off and leave the lounge. Surprisingly, the instructors were pretty much hands off the rest of that night. I left, went back up to the barracks, and went to sleep. I had a busy morning ahead of me.

The next morning at around 0500, we were downstairs in formation. We marched over to the mess hall, sounded off with the Ranger Creed, and knocked out our pull-ups. Well, sort of.

We were all pretty weak, so we all helped each other out by lifting one another's legs so that we could knock out six. It was our last breakfast and meal all together at the Camp Rudder dining facility. Scrambled eggs, hash browns, and sausage, with some pancakes to boot! Damn, that was awesome food!

After breakfast, we were to draw our weapons from the arms room and begin cleaning them. That was our entire task for that day until it was time to leave and fly back to Fort Benning, Georgia. Our duffle bags and rucksacks were already packed, and our uniforms were washed and cleaned. I had a little task before cleaning weapons. Actually, so did my entire squad. The senior RI came out of the headquarters and called for me and then told the entire squad to march over on their own and stand by outside until he came out and got them.

I went inside and reported to the company commander. I stopped in front of his desk, conducted a left face, saluted him and sounded off with, "Sir, Roster Number Five-Zero reporting as ordered, sir!"

He returned the salute and replied, "At ease, Ranger. Roster Number Five-Zero, do you know why you are before this board this morning?"

"Yes, sir."

"It says here that your squad peered you low. Do you have any reason why they would, Ranger?"

"Yes, sir, I believe they're upset with me because on Santa Rosa Island, I was yelling at the platoon leader to go after and lead the assault element on the raid. For whatever reason, sir, he refused to do anything. I finally physically grabbed his LCE and pushed him out to follow them, sir. Had he not gone with them, I was going to take over his duties as PL, and put the weapons squad leader in charge of the CCP and the prisoner guards, in order to oversee the completion of our mission, sir."

The CO came back with, "OK, Ranger, that's pretty much what Sergeant So-and-So [the RI] told me happened out there. You pretty much helped Roster Number So-and-So receive a passing grade. OK, Sergeant, call in Roster Number Five-Zero's squad."

When the squad filed in, they were instructed by the captain to stand directly behind me.

"OK, Five-Zero, you're going to turn around and your squad is going to tell you why each one of them peered you last."

"Roger, sir," I replied. I did an about-face and stood at the position of attention. The CO ordered me to stand at ease. He then asked the squad to raise their hands if they would follow me in combat and if they believed I was tactically and technically proficient. I couldn't wait for this reaction. As I thought, every hand in the squad went up. Starting from the left, each member was to tell me their reasoning for their decision.

The first student went ahead. "I peered you last because you became out of control on the final objective and physically put your hands on Roster Number So-and-So, and I believe that was unnecessary."

"Roster Five-Zero, go ahead and respond to your classmate, Ranger," the commander ordered.

I looked at him very humbly and said, "I understand your frustration, but it was combat, number one. Number two, had I not forced him to follow and lead the assault element, he definitely would have been a No-Go on the mission. That's why I did what I did." He just nodded, almost in agreement.

The next member of the squad said to me, "I peered you last because, well, I mean, well, somebody has to be last."

The commander slammed his fist down on his desk and began yelling at the top of his voice.

"What the fuck kind of answer is that, Ranger? Somebody has to be fucking last? That is not a legitimate reason under any circumstance to peer anybody in this fucking school last!"

He was pissed!

"Roster Number Five-Zero, turn around and face me!"

I did an about-face.

"Ranger, I think I know what's going on here. I've seen this kind of shit before. You're going back to Fort Benning this afternoon with the rest of the class to graduate in a couple of days. You are dismissed, Ranger, and good luck to you."

I saluted him and said, "Rangers lead the way, sir!"

He returned the salute and replied, "All the way!" I conducted a left face and marched out of his hooch. He didn't even wait for me to fully leave before he began yelling at the squad. When I got outside, the senior instructor was waiting on me.

"Remain cool, and don't do anything that's going to keep you here, Ranger. Good job and congratulations." I shook his hand and thanked him—"Roger, Sergeant"—and moved out to clean our weapons.

When the squad came out and linked back up with the platoon, which was about a half hour later, it was pretty quiet at first. I couldn't hold back anymore and had to say my piece, but did it calmly.

"Your little plot against me backfired on your sorry asses, didn't it?"

They didn't say shit back to me.

I finished by telling them, "This is the last thing I'm going to say to you shit-bags. Don't ever let me catch you out there in the real Army after this school. It ain't gonna be pretty, boys. I'm done with y'all." There, I had said my piece to their sorry faces. Hell, I don't even think but a couple of them even left. I believe the majority of them were recycled again. Like *Forrest Gump* used to say, "That's all I have to say about that."

After we turned in our weapons for the final time, we went upstairs and got our duffle bags. We came back downstairs with our gear, and I walked right back to my original company and platoon. I didn't even ask; I just did it. Fuck it. Nobody said shit, either. I was back with my platoon from Darby and Mountains again. It was like a little reunion. We all sat down on our bags and waited on the buses to take us to the airfield.

CHAPTER 8

BACK TO CAMP ROGERS
AND GRADUATION

When we got to the main airfield on Eglin, a couple of C-130s were already waiting there to fly us back to Fort Benning. We loaded all of our duffle bags in the center, piled up and stacked our rucks in another pile. This was going to be a simple, short airplane ride back, and without parachuting, either. I guess previous classes used to jump back into Benning, but for whatever reason they just had us landing. Probably since we had our duffle bags. They were cutting back on the logistical aspect of trucking them from Florida back to Georgia. Maybe budget cuts. I mean, we were at war during this time. Anyway, we were all OK with that. I don't even think it was an hour flight, but it was going to be a nice little nap anyway. I sat next to Germany, and we were shooting the shit, but once the bird took off, it was nighty-night time again.

When we landed back at Benning, there were buses waiting to take us back to Camp Rogers. As we rode back, I remember looking out the window and thinking how much I missed this post but couldn't wait to leave it either. We drove around a corner and there it was, all in black and gold lettering—Camp Rogers, 4th RTB. The buildings were all painted in black and gold as well, just like we remembered. We had made it back!

The bus stopped in front of the entrance of the camp, and the RI stood up and said, "Alright, Rangers, get your duffle bags and rucks and get into formation out in front of the headquarters."

As we walked back inside the camp, another formation was standing there—a platoon getting ready to ship to Mountain Phase. One of the students was a Bat Boy who had been in our original class that started two months ago, and he was just now finally leaving Benning. Wow! We walked by him and gave him high-fives. I remember thinking he must have been on one of those nine or ten-month Ranger School programs. Fuck that! Sixty-two days was enough for me.

Another instructor came out of headquarters and said to us, "Congratulations, Rangers, you made it!" We were told that the chow hall was opened for lunch and that we were to march over, knock out the Ranger Creed and our pull-ups, eat and get back on our equipment for further instructions. Everybody cheered and clapped their hands. We marched over and attempted to knock out six pull-ups. I stress the word *attempted* because I could barely do one. My body had been so depleted of strength. I had Germany grab my legs and assist me with six. I then helped him knock out his six. He was skinnier than I was. He was already tall and slim when we started.

After chow, we went back to formation, and the RIs instructed us to move our stuff back to our original barracks and begin cleaning our equipment, because the next morning was equipment turn-in at CIF—Central Issue Facility. We all cheered and clapped again! Everybody was so excited. We moved back, cut all the tie-offs on our equipment, and scrubbed everything down outside of the barracks. We then hung everything to dry in the sun.

After we got back from CIF the next morning, we were marched across the street to the hand-to-hand pit. I remember thinking, *What the fuck, are we going to start this shit again?* We were under the impression that they were going to make us do some more fighting, bear crawls, and buddy carries. Shit, I had no damn strength for that crap.

Nope! It was our class graduation picture. They had set up bleachers underneath the hanging Ranger Tab at the entrance of the fighting pit. We were told to load them with tall on top and the shorter Rangers towards the ground.

At last, it was the morning of graduation day! After our last meal at the chow hall (like there were so many—that's sarcasm), me and Germany went back up to the company headquarters. There we received our manila folders. Inside were our orders for our new skill identifiers of "V," which meant Airborne Ranger; also, our orders that awarded us the Ranger Tab; and a Fort Benning training certificate for successfully completing US Army Ranger School. Lastly, they also gave us copies of our jump logs that showed our two jumps during the course, to take back to our units with us. I was then given back my set of keys to my truck. It's funny because up until that point, I had damn near forgotten that I drove myself to the school two months ago, and that I had a vehicle there.

We went back to the barracks, got our duffle bags, and loaded them into my truck. If you had a privately-owned vehicle (POV) at the school, you were, of course, authorized to drive yourself to the graduation ceremony. After that, it was goodbye to Ranger School. Germany was going to ride with me. His flight didn't leave for Germany until the next day. So, the plan was to have lunch at an-all-you-can-eat restaurant, and then I was going to drop him off at a hotel in Columbus (just outside of Fort Benning). I figured I'd better start my truck to ensure it was going to start after two months, and it did. I let it run for a little while. He and I went back to the barracks to help finish cleaning and mopping it. An RI came in and did a quick inspection and then told us we were good to go. I believe the graduation ceremony was at 1000. It was at Victory Pond (where we conducted the water obstacle course two months ago).

Our company had one last formation at Camp Rogers, and then it was time to go. We were released to our POVs, and those that didn't have one loaded on the buses that pulled up in front of the company headquarters. Me and Germany pulled out of Camp Rogers and high-fived each other. Off to Victory Pond we went. I was to not only graduate and leave, but also see my family again. My wife was bringing our two kids, along with my uncle, who lived outside of Fort Bragg. A couple that we were friends with from back when I was a drill sergeant were coming over from Fort Rucker, Alabama, which was about fifty miles away from Benning. The husband was assigned there as the first sergeant at the US Army Warrant Officer Academy.

When we arrived to the graduation site, we parked and ran to get into formation, just underneath the big demonstration rappel tower that was painted all black with a big Ranger Tab on it—pretty intimidating. We formed up as one large class—I would say about eighty new Rangers. The RIs came through and handed each of us our Ranger Tabs, already with a safety pin through them, ready for the ceremony.

"Put them in your pockets, Rangers. Don't lose them. We don't have extras!" The plan was to meet and greet our friends and families, and go back to the bleachers with them to watch the demonstration that the RIs put on for the audience. It actually was very impressive, especially for the families. My poor uncle was a Vietnam veteran, and when the explosions went off during one of the demonstrations, he almost hit the ground. My wife and friends couldn't believe how much weight I had lost, either. I told them I weighed 142 pounds. We had a scale in our latrine at the barrack in Camp Rogers, and we all weighed ourselves. I got there at 170 pounds two months ago.

After the show, we formed back up into our class formation, and we had our friends or family members pin our tabs on our shoulders. It was quite emotional. Afterwards our families went back to the bleachers, and the Ranger Training Brigade commander had all of us say the Ranger Creed one last time. He then said the magic words, "Ranger School Class 11-03—DISMISSED!" We all started screaming and made a mad-dash sprint to the lake, and we all dove in. Fuck it!

Let's all get wet in Ranger School one last time, right? Yeah, we had planned it when we first formed up.

Afterwards, Germany and I went back to my truck, my family and friends met us there, and we discussed the plan for lunch. Germany and I had to change into dry civilian clothes first, and then we would all carpool off post to the Golden Corral in Columbus. Once everyone took off, we changed right there outside my truck, and we did it quickly. We were secluded out by the wood line, but there were still some people leaving. We didn't care; we were thinking about Golden Corral. We then drove out of the parking lot of Victory Pond. On November 7, 2003, we graduated from the United States Army Ranger School and earned our Ranger Tabs.

Inside Golden Coral, of course we each ate like we were going to prison the next day. Like we were going to the electric chair. Like it was our last meal. Like someone was going to take it from us. Like we were the shark eating the little boy on the raft in *Jaws*. There, I think I said all my eating analogies throughout this book.

We must have made three trips apiece through the buffet, and each time we came back to the table with something different. As we ate our food, we hardly said two words between us or to my friends and family. Then it was time for dessert. We got a little of everything there as well, to include ice cream. Wow, we were stuffed.

After the restaurant, I took him to his hotel. I got out of the truck and helped him carry his duffle bags inside the lobby. They were so heavy. We were both weak from what we had been through for the past two months. We gave each other one last hug and said our goodbyes.

"You take care of that daughter of yours when you get back home, brother," I said to him.

"Oh yeah, will do, man. You make sure you take care of yourself and be safe in Iraq."

"Oh yeah, too easy," I replied.

He looked at me and said the magic phrase—"Way too fucking easy." That was it. I never saw my Ranger buddy again. He was a great guy and I wish him all the best.

What an experience, that I wouldn't change for anything. I made it through the toughest combat training course on the planet. I could accomplish anything after that. I am so proud to have served with such warriors. The instructors are some of the most professional trainers in the military. Of course, there were a couple of bumps in the road for me, but so there are for almost every other student that volunteers for this school. Less than 1 percent of the Army is Ranger qualified. Out of that, only approximately 25 percent of each class will make it straight through. I am so proud to have achieved that elite status during my military career. The best weight-loss program on the planet, and I made it through.

After almost six months of extensive training between ANCOC and Ranger School back-to-back, Fort Benning was finally in my rearview mirror, but my journey ahead was just beginning. As I looked out the window on our road trip back to Fort Bragg, North Carolina, reality set in. I was heading straight to combat as soon as I checked back in with the rear-detachment element of my battalion. The enemy on the streets in the southern outskirts of Baghdad couldn't really care less whether or not I was Ranger qualified; they were going to try to kill me regardless. Two weeks later, I arrived and linked up with my unit at Forward Operating Base Saint Michael in Mumuhdyah, Iraq, and immediately began conducting and leading combat operations. This time, it wasn't with blank rounds. It was with live bullets.

Stay tuned; I have more stories to tell you.

Sign outside of Camp Rogers

Where it begins . . . and where it ends

Entrance to the hand-to-hand combat area at Camp Rogers

Rope Corral knot-tying test—Camp Merrill

Rock climbing lane
at Mt. Yonah

Mt. Yonah, Mountain Phase mountaineering "uppers" portion–
area rappelling and rock-climbing cliffs

Boat movement Florida Phase. The RI sits in the back to oversee. Notice the walking stick he holds.

Swamp movement Florida Phase.
Hours of enduring "the suck"

My original Ranger
Handbook after
all these years.
Found it after I
finished writing the
manuscript for this.

Our class picture the day before graduation. I am fourth row up,
third Ranger in from the right. Germany was top row,
also third in from the right.

Our graduation ceremony. I was in front of the formation, next to the
company guide-on (flag). Afterwards, when we were dismissed by
the Ranger Training Brigade commander, we all jumped in Victory
Pond behind us.

November 7, 2003, Sergeant First Class Nathan Aguinaga—
Roster Number Five-Zero. At age thirty-one, I earned my tab
and was thirty pounds lighter than sixty-two days before, when
we began the course. Too easy!

AKNOWLEDGMENTS

I would like to give my special thanks to my wife, Jessica, who continues to encourage me to write these stories down that I have been sharing with her for over a decade now, and also to you, my readers. Also, to my two children, Madyson and Taylor, for their continuing support of everything I do. I would like to thank my friends and family that purchased my first book, *Division*, along with the men and women of Koehler Books for making both these books a reality for me, and an easy process to publish. Also, to the community of North Baltimore, Ohio, for their continuing support. Particularly, my buddies Joe, Jim, and John Stewart for not only being good friends that will do anything for me, but also for giving me funny quotes from our meals, such as, "Jesus, you're not going to prison," or "Hey, man, nobody's going to take it from you." Awesome! Thank you, gentlemen. Finally, to ALL the Rangers across all of the branches of the military both past and present. Rangers Lead the Way.